"If, by some quirk of fate, all players suddenly refrained from making proposition bets, betting the Big 6 and Big 8, field bets, and place numbers, and everyone consistently made only line bets with maximum odds, the casinos might very well close up their dice tables. A .6% house advantage would not pay the salaries and other expenses incurred in running the games. Now, we wouldn't want that to happen—we'd have nowhere to play. So to all those uninformed, thrill-seeking players out there . . . keep those chips a-flying!"

DEDICATION

I dedicate this book to my loving wife and best friend
Nancy whose continuous support throughout this
project was indispensable and also to our wonderful
children Leigh, Alex, Katie and Collin for their
patience, interest, and support.

SPECIAL THANKS

A very special thanks goes to Mark Ewald and to
my sister Dr. Suzanne Roto Lake, for their
literary expertise and advice.

ACKNOWLEDGMENTS

I would also like to acknowledge the following for
their contributions: Phil Tatum, Damencele DiPasqua,
Anita Mrozinski, Chris Crane, and Allan Wilson.

COVER DESIGN BY:

Michael McConville

Table of Contents

Contents

Preface

Michael enters the casino. He experiences an immediate sensory rush of sight and sound. He cranes his neck, surveying the floor, looking for "his" game. "Out! Seven out!" he hears from a distance—the perennial cry of the Stickman. Michael's ears prick up like a bloodhound hot on the trail. He is quickly off to the craps tables.

As he approaches, his heart pounds and his hands begin to sweat. The tables are full and people are screaming. As he begins to circle the pit, he sees a stogy old cigar smoker slam his hand down hard and twist away from the rails in disgust. He sees a beautiful blond dressed in black, adorned with gold jewelry, accompanied by her martini-sipping escort. She lets out a scream as she flings the dice across the table. At the same time, a group of college rowdies jump up and down, slapping high fives as if they just scored in the final two minutes of the big game.

Michael spots a small opening and squeezes in. He reaches into his pocket and pulls out a hundred-dollar bill as he pokes his head out over the action. He reaches to hand the note to the standing dealer and says, "four twenty-five dollar chips, please."

"Set it down, sir," the dealer snaps. With that, the dice fly—one crashing down on a pile of chips, the other careening off Michael's hand.

"Hands up!" one of the players barks. Michael drops the hundred and quickly retracts his hand.

Poor Michael. He has been at the table less than fifteen seconds and he has already made a number of mistakes, some critical and some just plain embarrassing.

For one thing, he should have known that all casinos have firm policies prohibiting players from giving or receiving chips or cash directly to or from the hand of a dealer. If this is done, the dealer's employment can be terminated and the gambler can be ejected from the grounds.

Casinos can be very generous with perks and benefits. These are called "comps" (short for complimentary). Comps can only be earned if you ask for them, and this allows the casino to rate your play. Casinos issue small plastic cards, like credit cards, to players that want to be rated. It is essential to show this card every time you begin play at a table—another thing Michael does not know. But don't worry, his embarrassment will be short-lived. Betting twenty-five dollar chips with a total of only one hundred dollars in play, it is highly unlikely, statistically speaking, that Michael will last for more than a few minutes.

Michael loves the action and can hardly wait to play. However, like the vast majority of gamblers, and particularly craps players, Michael is a consistent loser. He does not understand why it feels like the dice always go against him. It seems to him that other players are doing just fine. Michael can remember a couple of years ago when he went to the tables with just a few dollars and walked away with a thousand. It's this memory, along with his hopes and prayers that it will happen again, that keeps him coming back.

He has thought about trying to learn the craps game the right way. He fantasizes about gaining some kind of edge over the house. But he has little time for research. Of the few books he found on gaming, some included a section on casino craps, but they also included a dozen other games that he has no interest in or didn't even recognize...what the hell is Pai gow poker?! What Michael needs is a short, easy-to-read book devoted exclusively to casino craps. A book that is up to date and clearly explains today's game, along with basic, sound gambling tenets that genuinely—statistically—give the player the very best chance of winning. A book that not only allows him to learn the game fast, but can also be used as a reference to deepen his understanding as time goes on. Perhaps most importantly, he needs a book that was written by a professional who has documented his winnings over the years, proving the value of his techniques.

CASINO CRAPS: *Strategies for Reducing the Odds Against You* is a book that finally addresses the specific needs of the countless gamblers who share Michael's predicament.

Introduction

Casino craps is an amazing, exciting game. It's the fastest game in the casino. When played correctly, it offers the player the very best chance of winning of any game in the casino.

Large amounts of money move quickly around the craps table at lightning speed—with most of it flowing into the casinos' bankroll. This is because very few people know how the game is best played, and even those that have taken the time to study it frequently ignore their knowledge and make foolish bets. These bets may be exciting, with large potential payoffs, but they give the house an outrageous advantage that could never be overcome in any medium or long-range time frame. Casinos are predatory in nature and count on these thousands upon thousands of people who are all too willing to pull out money, lose it, pull out more, and quickly lose that. This need not be the case.

You can get basic craps betting and percentages anywhere; here you will get much deeper tutelage than that. We will cover all bets available at the table with a complete and simplified analysis. This book is about professional play, bet patterns, bet progressions, money management, and winning with fair consistency.

When played in an optimal way, casino games reveal a correlation between the complexity of the game and the amount of skill required on the one hand, and the potential house advantage on the other hand. Consider the following:

Slots (virtually no skill)	6%–17% House Advantage
Roulette Double Zero (some skill)	5.26% House Advantage
Baccarat (high skill)	1.06% House Advantage
Black Jack (higher skill)	<1.0% House Advantage*
Craps (most complex)	.6% House Advantage

*without counting cards

As with most things in life, the more time and effort expended and the greater the understanding achieved, the greater the reward. And with proper bet patterns, bet progression, and money management, a .6% house advantage can be overcome. We are going to take the complexity and mystery out of the game of craps and explain it in clear, organized, understandable terms, all laid out in a very actionable format.

What must one do to become a winner at this game? Maybe you've heard a few friends tell you their disjointed thoughts and fragmented theories on the game, knowing full well they lose most of the time. Maybe the casino personnel have offered their help on how to play. By the time you finish reading this book, you'll have a professional overview with the best play strategies available. With a little practice you'll be prepared to meet the casino on virtually equal terms with the very best chance to win!

There are two ways to play this game: 1) for the thrill of high stakes action and the dream of making a fortune, or 2) for the purpose of making money with a professional's eye on statistical correctness and disciplined money management. 98% or 99% of all gamblers fall into the first category. These players are not willing to spend the little time necessary to really learn this game and to apply the proper tenants once at the table. They simply want action and entertainment and they get it with dice. The problem is that it becomes very expensive action and entertainment when play is left to hunches, hot tips, gut feelings, and chance.

This book is written for those who not only want to fall in the second category of calculated success, but also are willing to invest the little time necessary to learn and practice correct play. These are the players who will be feared by the casino personnel because they can intelligently fight them at their own game. The best way to become popular with the casino personnel is to ignore the strategies outlined in this book. They'll smile big as you walk up and make you feel right at home. They'll serve you drinks and cajole you while you're taking a financial beating. Then they'll pat you on the back and tell you "better luck next time" and quickly turn their attention to the next pigeon. They'll take all you got with no regard for your personal situation. I've never seen a floorman or a dealer say "Hey, buddy, I think you've had enough". They'll take everything and wish it had been more.

Don't let this happen to you. I've studied the game of craps synoptically. I've studied the work of some very good gaming experts and some very bad ones. I've practiced and played and refined these winning concepts for years. It is not immodest to say I am a lifetime winner at casino craps. I want to share my knowledge and experience with you and give you the best chance of being a winner.

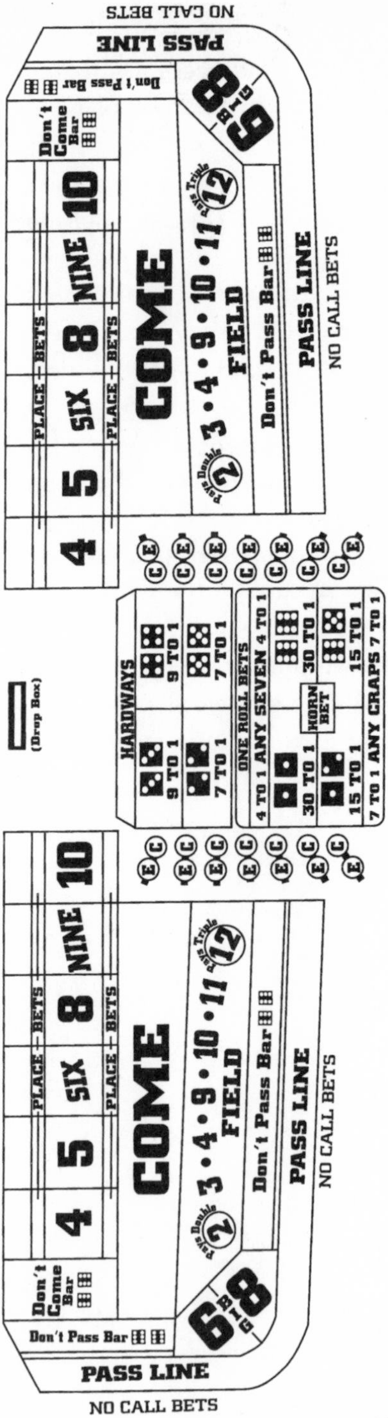
NO CALL BETS
PASS LINE
Don't Pass Bar
Don't Come Bar
4
5
SIX
8
NINE
10
PLACE — BETS
PLACE — BETS
COME
Pays Double 2
3 • 4 • 9 • 10 • 11
Pays Triple 12
FIELD
Don't Pass Bar
PASS LINE
NO CALL BETS
BIG 6 8
C E
(Drop Box)
HARDWAYS
9 TO 1
9 TO 1
7 TO 1
7 TO 1
ONE ROLL BETS
4 TO 1 ANY SEVEN 4 TO 1
30 TO 1
30 TO 1
HORN BET
15 TO 1
15 TO 1
7 TO 1 ANY CRAPS 7 TO 1
Don't Come Bar
4
5
SIX
8
NINE
10
PLACE — BETS
PLACE — BETS
COME
Pays Double 2
3 • 4 • 9 • 10 • 11
Pays Triple 12
FIELD
Don't Pass Bar
PASS LINE
NO CALL BETS
Don't Pass Bar
BIG 6 8
PASS LINE
NO CALL BETS

CHAPTER ONE

The Basics

Undoubtedly, anyone interested in reading a book on casino craps has at least approached a craps table and for a few moments observed the players and the action. Many are intimidated by the table with its fast action and players shouting out their bets, all to the incessant play-by-play calls of the stickman. Even the layout of the felt would appear, at first glance, impossible to understand.

As with most things in life, a little education and familiarity will go a long way in allaying fears and clearing the way for great things.

The Table

All craps tables are essentially the same. The standard table is twelve feet long by three and a half feet wide. It is a heavy wooden structure with a comfortably padded leather arm or resting rail to accommodate the players. Some players have been known to play non-stop for 6, 12, even 18 hours or more. If this is your style of play the casino will want you to be as comfortable as possible. They know that this kind of compulsive play is destructive to the player and they'll do what they can to encourage it.

On one side of the table there is a deep cut out section that accommodates two standing dealers and the boxman. On the other side is a smaller cut out section for the stickman. These personnel will be discussed individually shortly. Running the length of the padded arm rests are wooden troughs perfectly suited to hold the player's chips. There are twenty-two sections. Theoretically, this would serve twenty-two players, but only if they are 129 pounds each and standing sideways. Usually a table is full when between fourteen and eighteen players are present. It takes only one player with some money and a desire to make some more to get things going, and a full crew is required to service even that one player.

The Pit, The Crew, and Casino Personnel

Usually the casino will arrange eight tables in an oval or oblong configuration that encircles the area called the "pit". This configuration gives the casino maximum control over all eight tables. Players are not allowed inside the pit except on very rare occasions.

When a player approaches the table he'll see three standing dealers and one seated person called the boxman. The crew consists of four dealers; two flanking the boxman, one, called the stickman, directly across from the boxman, and one on break. The crew works straight through an eight-hour shift and circulates or switches positions around the table every twenty minutes. For example, the stickman will move to the position left of the boxman, the dealer who occupied that position will move to the right of the boxman, the dealer who occupied that position will go on break, and the dealer who was on break will replace the stickman. Twenty minutes later, the rotation occurs again, and so on. All this is done without interrupting the game; some players won't even notice it.

This continues for eight hours. Three full eight hour shifts makes twenty-four hours and the game is indeed played twenty-four hours a day, and seven days per week, and 365 days per year. Craps tables make casinos a lot of money, especially from the unaware. To close a table at any time is to forego income.

Functions of The Stickman

He is called the stickman because of the long flexible stick he holds to manipulate the dice around the table. After the dice are thrown he'll call out the numbers as well as the effects on some of the bets. For example, if on a come out roll the dice come up seven, he might call out "seven, a winner! Pay the line!" Or, after a point is established and a seven is thrown, he might say "Out! Seven out! Line away!" indicating that all the pass line bettors have lost. A five might prompt the call "Five! A no field five!" Indicating that this is a losing roll for the field bettors. There is no standard or required language. His job is to simply talk up the game, add to the excitement, and continually remind players of the proposition bets that lie directly in front of him in the center of the table. The center or proposition bets are also his domain and as chips are thrown into the center of the table by betting players he organizes them in the various boxes. He also directs the two standing dealers to pay off those players who have won on the center bets. The pace of the game is largely controlled by the stickman. He'll hold the dice until all bets are attended to and then he'll push them back to the shooter to be thrown again. And so it goes.

The Standing Dealers

There are two standing dealers, one on each side of the boxman. When a player first arrives at the table, the dealer nearest to him should greet him. The job of each standing dealer is to directly interact with the players and pay off or collect on all bets made on their respective halves of the table. Each side of the table layout is identical to the other, so working one side is no different from working the other. Dealers will answer any questions you might have and are generally helpful and personable and can add to the enjoyment of the game. As with any profession, there are some dealers with bad attitudes. This can easily distract from the game. There is no need to play with a dealer who has a bad attitude. You're the customer and there are plenty of other tables and crews that will be happy to have you.

To begin play, a player will either toss cash on the table or request credit if he has it at the casino. Credit must be set up beforehand at the casino's in-house bank or cage, along with a thorough credit investigation. If the player has credit, the dealer will catch the attention of the floorman. The floorman will then ask the player how much credit he is requesting. Credit is usually given in increments of $500. The floorman then prepares the appropriate marker or I.O.U. for the player to sign. Once credit is approved and the marker is signed, the floorman will instruct the dealer to advance the appropriate number of chips to the player.

If the player does not desire credit he can merely pull out cash and motion to the dealer that he's requesting chips. The dealer will indicate to the player to set the money down in the large betting box marked COME. For security reasons dealers are forbidden to receive or hand cash or chips directly to or from the hand of a player. The dealer will pick the money up and place it in front of the boxman. The boxman will then count the money by laying it all out in an orderly fashion on the table in front of him. This is done for all to see, especially the security camera mounted in the ceiling above. He will then count out the appropriate number of chips from the large casino bankroll in front of him and slide them over to the dealer who will forward them to the player.

A player is not required to "check in" to a table to play. He might simply walk up to any table with a game in progress and place chips in a betting box. When the bet is determined a winner or loser, he can just pick up and walk away. This is known as a "fly by," and while it can be exciting and fun, it is not a serious way to play craps and I defy anyone to win over time by doing this.

The first roll of a game is called the "come out" roll. On the come out roll if a seven or eleven is rolled the dealer will payoff or collect on all appropriate bets. If "craps" is rolled (2,3 or 12) the dealer will also pay off or collect on all appropriate bets. If a "point" number is rolled (4,5,6,8,9 or 10) the dealer will take the black and white disk labeled "on" on one side and "off" on the other, and place it in the appropriate point number box with the white or "on" side up. This indicates that a game is in progress. The disk is called the Marker Puck. When the disk is "off" and the table is between games it is usually placed in the don't come box by the dealer.

When tables are busy, lots of bets of all types and sizes are being made by the players around the table, and the dice are crashing down and bouncing around, it might appear to be an unmanageable situation. But this is the dealers' job—to keep all the bets organized and to quickly and accurately pay off to the right players. Dealers are generally very well trained, especially in the bigger casinos, but mistakes do happen. Learn the proper bets and their proper payoffs so that you can immediately spot an error that's not in your favor and point it out to the dealer. Once the chips are returned to the rails it's too late to make corrections. Don't get shortchanged—ever.

The Boxman

The boxman is not part of the crew. He is seated facing the action of the table with his back to the pit. His job is to watch the dealers and all the action and to watch over the casino's bankroll at that particular table. If necessary, the boxman will mediate or settle any disputes that might arise during play between a player and a dealer. This doesn't happen too often and when it does, the boxman is usually fair in administering standard rules of play.

The Floorman

The floorman stands in the pit and oversees the boxmen and the action of perhaps two to four tables. His job is to see to it that the player's needs such as drinks, cigarettes, cigars, phone messages, etc. are tended to. They will also check a players play or "action" for complimentary status and answer other questions upon request. The floorman oversees the credit standings of those players who want credit and he is available to authorize credit on the spot. Further, if, after a dispute, a player is unsatisfied with the decision of the boxman, he can appeal to the floorman. The floorman is usually very player friendly—even more so than the boxman. The floormen (usually 2 to 4 to a pit) are watched by a single pit boss. The pit bosses are watched by the casino manager and everybody is watched by a network of overhead cameras operated by top ranking casino security personnel. These cameras are commonly referred to as the "Eye in the Sky". This is a longstanding integrated system of casino operations and security that in no way should effect your play or your ability to become a winner at this game.

The Layout

One look at a craps table layout (see page xx) is enough to cause many to give up on this casino wonder before even giving it a chance, despite the fact that, when played correctly, the game gives the player the very best odds of winning. If we systematically break down the various sections of the layout, things will quickly and clearly come in to view. The following is a standard Las Vegas craps layout.

As we can see, the layout is divided into three separate sections—two identical end sections and one center section containing the "hardway" and "proposition" bets. Each dealer flanking the boxman controls all the bets, payoffs and collections for his section of the table. The center section of the table is controlled by the stickman. All the bets that relate to these sections of the table will be discussed individually and at length in Chapters 3 and 4. Ultimately, we'll see that all center bets are bad bets as they give much too large an advantage to the house.

There are two bets that are not imprinted on the craps layout. Oddly enough, one of them, the "hop" bet, is the worst bet available to players, giving the house an obscene advantage, while the other one, the "free odds" bet, is not only the best bet available at the table but happens to be the best bet available at *any* game or machine in the casino! We will explore both these bets later and show how to exploit the free odds bet for maximum profitability.

Chapter Summary

Casinos are a high security environment with well-trained personnel, especially in the larger casinos. Tables are staffed by 4 dealers; 3 on duty with one on break. The dealers watch the players. The boxmen watch the dealers. The floormen watch the boxmen. The pit boss watches the floormen. The casino manager watches the pit boss and all are watched by the "Eye in the Sky". This is all done in a very orderly manner so as to not distract the players. Casinos can be likened to the Big Bad Wolf in Little Red Riding Hood—they dress up all nice and pretty while laying in wait to devour you financially. You, on the other hand, might look to them like Little Red Riding Hood, but in reality you'll turn out to be the Woodsman.

CHAPTER TWO

The Dice, Their Combinations and The Odds

An intimate knowledge of the game must begin with a thorough understanding of dice combinations and the resultant odds. The possible combinations determine all the odds and all the payoffs on the layout.

Dice and dice games have been around for literally thousands of years. The dice used in casinos today are very finely machined. They measure approximately 3/4″ per side and are as close to a perfect cube as modern technology will allow. Casino dice are usually red but some casinos use other colors such as green or blue. Whatever color they chose does not matter. You will notice that all casino dice are transparent. This allows casino personnel to more easily check weights or other imperfections of counterfeit dice that have been improperly introduced by the unscrupulous in an effort to interfere with truly random rolls, which are essential to the game.

Dice Combinations

A cube, of course, has six sides of equal size. Each die is numbered with spots to represent numbers one through six.

If one were to take a single die and drop it onto a table in such a way as to allow it to fall randomly, the odds or chance of any particular number, say for example the 2, showing is 1 in 6. You can also express this as 5 to 1. That is, one chance to be a two versus five chances to be something else. When two dice are thrown there are 11 possible numbers that will result; they are 2,3,4,5,6,7,8,9,10,11 and 12. If each die has six sides then the total number of possible combinations is 6 X 6 or 36. All 36 possible combinations will, of course, total one of the 11 numbers listed above. If the dice both come up with their 1 spot showing then the total is 2. If one comes up 3 while the other is 4, the total would be 7. Obviously a 1 and a 6 would also make 7, as would a 2 and a 5. Clearly, there are more ways for 7 to be made than for 2 to be made. Actually, there are more ways for the 7 to be made than any other number. The following chart illustrates the 11 possible totals that two dice can make, and the specific combinations that make these totals.

Number	Combination
2	1-1
3	1-2, 2-1
4	1-3, 3-1, 2-2
5	1-4, 4-1, 3-2, 2-3
6	1-5, 5-1, 2-4, 4-2, 3-3
7	1-6, 6-1, 2-5, 5-2, 3-4, 4-3
8	2-6, 6-2, 3-5, 5-3, 4-4
9	3-6, 6-3, 4-5, 5-4
10	4-6, 6-4, 5-5
11	5-6, 6-5
12	6-6

You'll notice the diamond shape of the combination column, indicating that there are more ways for the 7 to be rolled than any other number. There are 6 combinations of the dice that will total 7 while there are only four combinations that will total 5. The following chart simplifies the previous one, again showing the eleven totals that two dice can make, and now tallying the number of ways in which the two dice can combine to make these totals:

Number	Ways to Make
2	1
3	2
4	3
5	4
6	5
7	6
8	5
9	4
10	3
11	2
12	1

Odds

Odds are defined as the likelihood of one thing occurring rather than another in an event of indefinite outcome. The dice combinations and their probabilities of occurring in relation to each other determine all the bets on the layout, the odds of all the bets, and all the accompanying payoffs. This might sound a little complicated, but it's not, as you will see when you become familiar with the numbers.

In every possible bet on the layout, the house maintains an advantage over the player. This is so because the casino payoff is less than the actual odds would dictate. There is only one exception, and that is the bet called "free odds". This bet does not appear on the layout but is allowed on all casino craps games. It is the only bet in the casino in which the house holds no advantage. Shortly, we will learn how to exploit this bet to its maximum.

Basic Playing Procedure

All craps tables that are in action will post bet limits, and sometimes some other notes, on small, color-coded plastic cards inside the table and under each of the two standing dealers.

These cards might, for example, be red and state that the minimum bet is $5 and the maximum bet is $2,000. Casinos want to entice people to play, and many players are attracted to tables by low bet limits. However, as the tables fill with players the casino will start changing the cards to indicate different minimum and maximum wagers. A table might start the evening with posted bet limits of $10 minimum and $3000 maximum, and then they might raise the minimum to $25 and the maximum to $5,000 as the casino fills up.

It is essential to select the bet minimum appropriate for your personal financial situation and personality. That is to say that no one should ever play at a table that is over his head, or where he feels uncomfortable. This will be discussed further in Chapter 8, Bankroll and Money Management.

When a table opens, the stickman will take a tray of between 5 and 9 dice and dump them on the table in front of the player immediately to his left. This player becomes the "shooter" and all bets made on the layout are collected or paid off based on this shooter's roll. Anyone can elect not to throw the dice; the stickman will simply slide the dice to the next player to the left. The dice proceed clockwise around the table giving everyone a chance to shoot. Opting to throw, the shooter selects two of the dice and the stickman returns the remaining dice to the tray, putting them out of play. The shooter must be sure to handle the dice with only one hand and to keep them out over the table at all times.

Now the shooter throws the dice. He must throw them the length of the table to the opposite end with at least one die bouncing off the inside angular-shaped wall—this ensures a truly random bounce. If the roll is short or "weak," the boxman will usually allow the roll to count, but he will caution the shooter that the dice must reach the far end of the table as described above. If the shooter continues to throw short the boxman may give a more strict warning, or he may begin to disallow rolls. It is said that there are experts who can "pinch" or control the dice to produce a favorable roll. I've never met anyone who has this fabled talent, but this is essentially what the boxman is watching for. It is generally agreed that if both dice travel to the end of the table with at least one die careening off the wall, then controlling the outcome would is impossible.

I've seen some nasty exchanges between boxmen and players, with the boxman trying to "over-direct" the throws of a player. The boxman might say the tosses are "too high" or "too low," or he might demand that the shooter throw directly down the center of the table. Remember—you're the customer and there are many casinos that will be happy to take your action. As long as your throws are legal as described above, the floorman (the boxman's direct supervisor) should back you up and allow you to throw with your own style.

To shoot the dice you are required to make a "line" bet of at least the table minimum. A "line" bet is a bet made on the pass line or the don't pass line. Regardless of any other bets that you may have on the layout, a line bet is required to shoot the dice. This is so because if a player did not have a line bet at risk, and only had one of the many other bets made on the table, he might lose that bet and then be inclined to walk away from the table while the other players are in the middle of a game that depends on his rolls!

As long as a shooter's money remains at risk he is more likely to see the game through. Once having made a line bet the shooter then, at his own pace, throws the dice. The shooter will continue to throw the dice, with bets being collected or paid off on each roll, until he "sevens out". That is, until he throws a 7 after a "point" has been established, thereby being a loser on the pass line. Line bets are integral to the game and will be discussed in full in the next chapter.

All major casinos will have at least one craps table open 24 hours a day, 365 days per year.

As the casino gets busy more tables will open. At peak time, weekend nights, and holidays, after all tables are in full operation, the management will begin to raise the minimum bets to insure that maximum play is always at hand.

Chapter Summary

The two dice can make thirty-six combinations. These thirty-six combinations can total eleven different sums. The probability of each of these combinations appearing on the dice determines all the odds and payoffs on all the bets. The house maintains an advantage on all the bets by paying less than the actual odds would dictate, with the exception being the free odds bet. The key number in craps is the seven, as there are more ways for the dice to make the seven than any other number. A player only needs a little cash and a table with play in progress to play. The stickman will move the dice clockwise around the table and anyone can throw the dice providing they have made a line bet.

CHAPTER THREE

Pass Line/Don't Pass and "Free Odds" (The Main Game)

The Pass Line Bet

The game of craps is based primarily around the pass line wager. It is estimated that a full 90% of all players play the pass line, yet it is rare to find a player either skillful, knowledgeable, or disciplined enough to consistently make this bet yield maximum returns over time.

I have played next to literally thousands of pass line players. So many times, at the same table, betting on the same rolls of the dice, I've walked away a winner while they broke even or lost their bankroll. This is usually a function of these players not maximizing their returns, or throwing their winnings away on silly and disadvantaged bets.

You'll find the pass line betting area is a long, narrow bar wrapping around many other bets at each end of the table. The words "pass line" are printed in this area. The pass line spans such a long area so as to be as easily accessible to all players at all positions around the table.

A pass line bet is an even money bet that can only be made on the first or starting roll of a game. This roll is called a "come out" roll. The marker puck will have its black side up, reading "off," usually resting in the don't come box. The stickman might call out "We're coming out! Get your line bets down," or some version of that. All other rolls of the dice are simply called come rolls. On the come out roll, if either a 7 or 11 is rolled then the pass line is an instant winner. The dealers will pay off all pass line bets at even money by placing the matching number of chips next to all pass line bets. The 7 and 11 are called "naturals" or "natural winners" when thrown on a come out roll. After the dealers pay off the pass line bets, the marker puck remains "off" and the next roll will be a come out roll again.

If, on the come out roll, a 2, 3, or 12 is rolled, this would be an immediate loser for the pass line bettor. The dealers will quickly collect all pass line bets. 2, 3 and 12 are called "craps," as the game itself is called. The marker puck will again remain "off" and we'll be coming out yet again.

Point Numbers

If any number other than the 7 or 11 (naturals) or 2, 3, or 12 (craps) is thrown on the come out roll, then that number becomes the shooter's "point". The dealer will immediately flip the disc to "on" with the white side up, and place it in the box of the point number that was rolled. This designates that number as the point and indicates that the game is now "on." Point numbers are the numbers 4, 5, 6, 8, 9 and 10.

Now, for the shooter to win, the point number must be thrown *before* the 7 is thrown. That is to say, if the point is thrown again (repeats), then the pass line bets are declared winners and are paid off at even money. In this case the dice are said to have "passed" or won.

If a seven is rolled before the point, this would be an immediate loser for the pass line bettor. The dealers will quickly collect all pass line bets. In this case, the dice would be said to have "not passed" or to have lost. The marker puck will again be put to "off" and we'll be coming out again.

Pass Line
On The Come Out Roll

7 or 11 (natural)	Win even money
2, 3 or 12 (craps)	Lose even money
4,5,6,8,9,10 (Point)	Must be repeated before 7 to win even money

NOTE: The only numbers that have an effect on the pass line bet *after* a point has been established are the 7 (to lose the bet) or the point itself (to win the bet). The following examples will illustrate the effects of various dice rolls on pass line betting:

1. Come out—7 (natural, instant win)
2. Come out—3 (craps, instant loss)
3. Come out—8 (point, following come rolls are 6, 12, 11, 9, 4, 8; win at even money)
4. Come out—5 (point, following come rolls are 11, 12, 2, 9, 3, 6, 10, 7; lose bet)

Let's briefly examine these examples. In example one, the 7 is thrown on the come out roll so the pass line bettor wins instantly and is paid off at even money. The disk remains "off" and the next roll is another come out roll. In example two a 3, or a craps, is thrown. All pass line bets are lost and collected by the dealers and the next roll is another come out roll.

In example three, an eight is rolled on the come out roll, thereby establishing the point for the table. The dealers flip their disks to white "on" and place them by the 8. The game is now "on". All rolls after a come out roll are called come rolls. In this case the first come roll is a 6. Where the 6 may effect other bets made on the table, it has no effect on the main game where, in this case, the point is 8. The next come roll is a 12 (craps) and again has no effect on our main game where the point is 8. The same goes for the following rolls of 11, 9 and 4. Finally, in example number three, the 8 is thrown, thereby repeating the point before the 7 had a chance to appear. This becomes a winning bet for the pass line, and all pass line bettors are paid at even money.

The disc goes "off" and the table is now set for another come out roll and the beginning of a new game.

In example number four above, a 5 is rolled on the come out roll and is thereby established as the point. The disk is flipped to "on" and placed by the 5. The following rolls of 11, 12, 2, 9, 3, 6 and 10 all have no effect. The pass line bettor awaits only the 5, which in this case wins, or the 7, which loses. In this example a 7 is rolled before the 5 is repeated, and this is a losing roll for our point 5. The dealers will collect up all bets—the disc will go "off" and a new shooter will hold the dice.

Pass Line
Bet Summary
Multiple Roll Bet
Placed by: The Player

On the come out roll

7 or 11 (natural): Wins even money

2, 3, or 12 (Craps): Loses

4, 5, 6, 8, 9 or 10 (points): Becomes the point

After point is established

Point number before 7: Wins even money

7 before point number: Loses

11: Neutral

2, 3, 12: Neutral

All other point numbers: Neutral

Special rules for pass Line bet: Can only be made on the come out roll and must be at or above the table minimum. Can not be taken down once a point has been established. Determines the amount of free odds that can be played.

House Advantage: 1.41%
Usefulness: Very useful—gaming based around this bet.

Free Odds

As mentioned earlier, the free odds wager is the most advantageous bet, not only at the craps table but also in the whole casino. This is so because it is the only bet available to the players where the house has no advantage. The free odds bets should be made 100% of the time when available and is the key to really big wins.

Interestingly, as one looks around the layout there is no indication of where or how to make the free odds bet or what it pays. But rest assured, every major casino offers this bet, and every intelligent, knowledgeable player should be able to exploit it to its fullest.

The free odds bet is available when a player makes a line bet, either pass line or don't pass, after the point has been established. (We'll cover don't pass betting in the next section). After a point is established the pass line bettor is allowed to make a bet of equal size to a free odds bet. To do this the player takes chips of equal denomination to the original bet and places them about two inches away from the bet nearer to himself or "behind the line". This is called a single odds game. Casinos today generally offer double odds, allowing the player to make a bet double his original wager behind the line which is definitely to the player's advantage. The uniqueness of this bet is that if it wins, that is to say the point repeats before the seven, it is paid off at true or correct odds! The following table shows the true or correct odds for each of the 6 point numbers 4, 5, 6, 8, 9, 10:

Free Odds Chart

Point No.	Ways to Make	Vs.	Ways to Make 7	Correct Odds	Casino Pays	House Adv.
4	3		6	2-1	2-1	0%
5	4		6	3-2	3-2	0%
6	5		6	6-5	6-5	0%
8	5		6	6-5	6-5	0%
9	4		6	3-2	3-2	0%
10	3		6	2-1	2-1	0%

As an example, let's look at the point number of 5. As we learned in Chapter 2, there are 4 combinations of the dice that will make a 5. If the point is 5 then any of these combinations will win even money for the pass line bet if thrown before the seven. However, the point of 5 loses if the 7 is rolled first. There are six combinations that make the 7. One can easily see that the odds of a 5 coming before a 7 are 6 to 4. This reduces down to 3 to 2. If the 5 is rolled the original bet is immediately paid off at even money, but the free odds bet is paid off at 3 to 2!

To further illustrate the free odds bet, let's say, for example, we bet $10 on the pass line. The point is then established as 5. We then make an odds wager of $10 more "behind the line" as our free odds wager. Now we have bet a total of $20. This would be called a single odds game, as our odds bet is the same size as our main bet.

If the 5 wins (repeats before the 7) the dealer will pay us $10—even money—for our pass line wager. However, our free odds wager of $10, made with odds of 3 to 2, wins us $15 on the same roll, for a total win of $25! Of course, the combined $20 we have wagered (10 on the the pass line bet and 10 on the odds wager) is subject to loss if the 7 is thrown first. The house edge on pass line gives it a 1.41% advantage over us, which is the lowest house advantage of all bets on the table except for the free odds bet itself. But when the pass line bet is followed with a single odds bet, the overall house advantage is reduced to .8 of 1%! And when double odds are played, the house edge falls to a mere .6 of 1%! This means that the player's loss expectation is a scant 60 cents for every $100 bet. These are the best odds available and are the key to your chances of making some money. These percentages and their meanings will be covered completely in the next chapter.

If the player were playing a double odds game in our example above, he would have simply made a $20 free odds bet behind his $10 pass line bet. Had the bet won, he would have been paid $30 on the odds wager ($20 at 3-2 odds yields $30 on a win) along with $10 at even money on the underlying pass line bet, for a total win of $40.

Now, re-examine the table on Page19. You'll notice that the table makes a sort of mirror image. That is, the odds are the same for the 4 and 10 (2-1), for the 5 & 9 (3-2), and for the 6 & 8 (6-5).

For further clarification, let's take the odds of the 7 coming before the 4 (or before the 10, which has an identical likelihood). There are 3 ways to make a 4: 1-3, 3-1, 2-2. With 6 ways to make a 7, we can represent the odds of a 7 coming before a 4 by comparing 6 possible combinations to 3 possible combinations, or "6 to 3," which reduces down to 2 to 1. If the point is a 4, the casino will pay off on the free odds wager, either single or double odds, at the correct 2-1 payoff. The casino therefore holds no advantage over the player.

It should be pointed out that for the sake of simplicity and ease of paying off, the casinos will allow the player to round up a little on the six and eight numbers when making the odds wager, whether the player is playing single or double odds. For example, if a $10 bettor is playing a double odds game he is allowed to make a $25 odds bet instead of a $20 bet on points of 6 or 8. With correct odds at 6 to 5, it is easier for the dealer to pay $30 on a $25 bet than it is for him to pay $24 on a $20 bet. This drops the over all house edge below .6 of 1% when done on a regular basis, and is definitely to the player's advantage. For clarity, all the examples in the following bet summary will incorporate straight single and double odds, but in actual play you should learn to round up when the point is six or eight.

Pass Line, Free Odds
Bet Summary
Multiple Roll Bet
Placed by: The Player
If Point Repeats

6 or 8:	Wins at 6 to 5
5 or 9:	Wins at 3 to 2
4 or 10:	Wins at 2 to 1
7:	Loses
11:	Neutral
2, 3, 12:	Neutral
Other Points:	Neutral
Special Rules:	The free odds wager can only be used in conjunction with a line bet in order to back up the line bet after a come out roll, were a point has been established. Size of bet is determined by the underlying pass line bet. Free odds can be taken down by the player at any time (but this should never be done)
House Advantage:	0.0%
Usefulness:	Very useful—should be used 100% of the time

Don't Pass Bar 12

As we've pointed out, it is estimated that 90% of craps players bet on the pass line. When one bets on the pass line he is said to be betting "with the dice". He might also be called a "right" bettor or a "do" bettor as he is betting that the dice will pass, either with a natural 7 or 11 on the come out roll or by establishing a point and then repeating that point before the 7 comes.

You'll notice on the layout the smaller betting area just above the pass line, marked "don't pass bar 12". With this bet the player is betting virtually the exact opposite of the pass line bettor. Consequently, this player is called a "don't" bettor or a "wrong" bettor as he is now betting "against the dice," which is to say he is betting that the dice don't pass. The title "wrong" bettor is quite the misnomer because if played correctly, the don't pass bet can be just as profitable as the pass Line.

On the come out roll the don't bettor wins even money instantly if a 2 or 3 is rolled, loses if the 7 or 11 turns up and if a point number is rolled, he will win if the 7 shows before the point is repeated. The overall advantage that the house maintains with the don't bet is 1.40%.

Bar 12

You'll recall that for the pass line bettor, a 2, 3, or 12 (craps) is a losing roll on the come out roll. However, for the don't pass bettor only the 2 and 3 are winning rolls on the come out. If the pass line and don't pass bets are opposites, why doesn't the 12 also win for the don't bettor? Above we said the don't pass bet was "virtually" the exact opposite as the pass line bet, and herein lies the difference. Simply stated, the 12 (on some layouts the 2) is barred from winning because if the 12 were allowed to be a winning roll for the don't pass bettor instead of a push, he would actually maintain an advantage over the house! This is what the words "Bar 12" refer to in the don't pass box. The 12 is barred from winning and instead is only a push with the house. With 36 combinations of the dice and only one of them equaling 12, the difference between a win versus a push is the difference between the house maintaining a 1.40% advantage on the one hand, and the player gaining an advantage over the house on the other hand. This illustrates how small the house advantage actually is. We will expound further on what this advantage means and how to best overcome it in the final chapters.

Don't Pass
Bet Summary
Multiple Roll Bet
Placed by: The Player
On come out Roll

2, 3:	Wins even money
7, 11:	Loses
12:	Push
4, 5, 6, 8, 9, 10:	Becomes the point

After a point is established

7 before point:	Wins even money
Point before 7:	Loses
Special rules:	Can only be made on the come out roll and must be at or above the table minimum. Can be taken down at any time even after a point has been established but this should never be done. (On the don't pass line, once a point is established the player has a distinct advantage over the house that should never be relinquished.)

House Advantage:	1.40%
Usefulness:	Very useful—gaming based around this bet

Free Odds on The Don't Pass Bet

The free odds bet is offered on the don't pass bet just as it is offered on the pass line bet, except it is played exactly opposite to the pass line free odds. Don't let this confuse you—it's really quite simple. Where the pass line bettor "takes" odds at no advantage to the house and is betting on the point repeating before the 7, the don't pass bettor "lays" odds at no advantage to the house and is betting on the 7 coming before the point. For example, let's say that on the come out roll the point is established to be a 9 and our original bet is $10. The odds of the 7 coming before the 9 are 3-2, in favor of the 7 of course.

Now, where our pass line bettor "takes" odds for $10 "behind the line" in hopes of winning $15 if the 9 comes before the 7, our don't pass bettor "lays" odds or bets $15 in hopes of winning $10 if the 7 comes first. Remember, the original bet of $10 is either lost or won at even money whether you're betting pass or don't pass.

So why would someone bet $15 to win $10 instead of betting $10 to win $15? This question is one reason why 90% of players play the pass line. However, laying odds on the don't pass line is equally advantageous to taking odds on the pass line. Remember, the 7 is 3 times to 2 more likely to show before the 9, making your lay odds wager more likely to win! In a double odds game, our $10 bettor would lay $30 to win $20 (instead of $15 to win $10) should the seven be rolled before the nine; the proportions stay the same at 3-2.

The following chart is a reiteration of the correct odds on all point numbers:

4 or 10	2-1
5 or 9	3-2
6 or 8	6-5

If the point were to come up 6 or 8 our $10 bettor would lay $12 to win $10, not the $15 that the 9 required, because the odds on the 6 or 8 are 6-5.

To make a free odds wager you place the appropriate number of chips next to your original bet in the don't pass area.

Don't Pass Free Odds
Bet Summary
Multiple Roll Bet
Placed by: The Player

7 before point:	4 & 10 win at 1 to 2
	5 & 9 win at 2 to 3
	6 & 8 win at 5 to 6
Point before 7:	Loses
Special Rules:	Can only be made after the come out roll where a point has been established, and only in conjunction with a don't pass bet. Size of bet is determined by the underlying don't pass bet. Can be taken down by the player at anytime (but this should never be done).

House Advantage:	0.0%
Usefulness:	Very useful—should be used 100% of the time

A Word about Free Odds

To help clarify just how advantageous to the player the free odds are, consider the following. Let's say that you and a friend were going to flip a coin 10 times and bet $10 on the outcome of each flip. Obviously, the odds of either the heads or the tails showing is 50-50 or, to put it in our odds terms, 1 to 1. To be on equal terms, you would win $10 each time the coin showed heads and your friend would win $10 each time the coin came up tails. This would be a fair bet and neither one of you would have an advantage over the other at the outset. Most likely you would end up breaking even after 10 flips of the coin. However, this would not necessarily be the outcome. The coin could come up 6, 7 or even 10 times on the same side, causing one of you to win more. Now, let's say the bet was this: every time the coin came up heads your friend wins $10, but every time the coin comes up tails you win only $9. First of all, this would explain why this guy wants to be your friend. With these terms your friend would maintain a 5% advantage over you, meaning he could expect to win $5 for every $100 bet. Now compare this to the casino's line bet advantage over you—only 1.4%— or the the casino's single odds advantage over you—only .8%— or its double odds advantage—a mere .6%.

In the above example you certainly could get lucky and the coin could come up tails 6 or more times and you would win. Six times $9 would gross you $54 against 4 losses totalling $40, for a net gain of $14. However, if you continued betting this way, that is you continued to give away a 5 percent advantage, you would lose over time.

Professional gamblers don't rely on luck. They take the time to learn the odds, then minimize the odds to a mere fraction and play the game's normal volatility to make long term gains with proper money management. This will be discussed in greater detail in Chapter 8.

The Come Bet

Craps players typically want action and lots of it. However, once a player has made a pass line bet and backs the point up with odds, there are only two of all 11 possible numbers that can affect the bet—the 7 for a loss or the point itself for a win. All other numbers are neutral. A player could wait a long time for his bet to be affected. To play just the pass line for hours on end, with the results of most rolls irrelevant to your bet, would not be the type of action one usually looks for as a craps player. Enter the come bet.

Within the configuration of bets on each end of the table is the large betting box prominently labeled "come". When betting "right," or with the dice, the come bet should be an integral part of the betting pattern. Once one understands the pass line bet, the come bet is easy. It is essentially the identical bet except for the issue of when it is made. The pass line bet is made when the disc is "off" (black in color) and the dice are "coming out" to establish the point. After the point is established, the right bettor can gain more action by making a come bet. To make a come bet, the player sets his chips in the come box. The next roll of the dice determines the fate of the come bet in a way identical to how the come out roll determines the fate of the pass line bet. That is, 7 or 11 (natural) wins; 2, 3, or 12 (craps) loses; and if the roll is a point number (4, 5, 6, 8, 9 or 10) the dealer will then take the come bet and place it in the point number box. Now the come bettor, in effect, has his own private game, with the same parameters and odds as the pass line bet—if the point repeats before the 7 he wins. If the 7 comes first, he loses.

The come bettor is also allowed to back up his bet with odds, just as with the pass line bet. To back up the come bet with odds, the player would toss the appropriate amount of chips in the come box and tell the dealer that the chips are the odds bet for the point just established. The dealer will then take the chips and set them on top of the bet that now sits in the point number box. To designate these chips as the odds bet, the dealer will set the chips atop but "off center" of the come bet. This way he'll know that if the bet wins by repeating the point number, he must pay off the odds bet at true odds while paying off the underlying come bet at even money.

Finally, the player may make as many come bets as he wishes. We'll discuss incorporating come bets into winning strategies, both conservative and aggressive, in Chapter 6 on bet patterns.

Come Bet
Bet Summary
Multiple Roll Bet
Placed by: The Player
First Come Roll

7 or 11 (natural):	Wins at even money
2, 3, or 12 (Craps):	Loses
4, 5, 6, 8, 9, or 10 (Points):	Becomes come point

After come point is established

Come point before 7:	Wins even money
7 before come point:	Loses
Other point numbers:	Neutral
11:	Neutral
2, 3, or 12:	Neutral
Special rules:	The come bet can only be made after the come out roll and after a point has been established. Come bets may be backed up with free odds identically to how the pass line bet is backed up. To bet free odds on come bet the player throws the appropriate number of chips in the come box and indicates to the dealer that the chips are "backing" up his come bet. Odds are "off" on come out rolls unless requested to be on by the player.
House Advantage:	1.41%
Usefulness:	Very useful

The Don't Come Bet

It is said that once someone has learned one foreign language it is substantially easier to learn subsequent languages, as most languages follow a pattern. Let's apply this analogy to the don't come bet. You'll notice the small betting box in the upper corner of the layout labeled "Don't Come Bar 12". Just as the come bet mirrors the pass line bet, the don't come bet mirrors the don't pass bet. The don't come bet is made after a point is established and has the same parameters as the don't pass bet. 7 or 11 loses, craps wins—except the 12, which is barred from winning for reasons we have covered, hence the words "Bar 12"— and if a point number is established then the 7 must come before the point to win.

Odds may now be laid, at correct odds, on the don't come bet, and are always working.

The don't come bet offers more action for the don't player and should be incorporated into the don't game bet pattern for maximum action and return of profits. Different strategies for don't play with varying degrees of aggressiveness with the don't come bets will be discussed in depth in Chapter 6.

Don't Come
Bet Summary
Multiple Roll Bet
Placed by: The Player
First Come Roll

2 or 3:	Wins even money
7 or 11:	Loses
12:	Push
Any other number:	Becomes point

After point has been established

7 Before don't come point:	Wins even money
Don't come point before 7:	Loses
Other Points:	Neutral
11:	Neutral
Special rules:	The don't come bet can only be made after a point has been established. Don't come bets may be backed up with free odds identically to how the don't pass bet is backed up. To bet free odds on the don't come bet the player throws the appropriate chips in the come box (or above the don't come box) and so indicates to the dealer.
House Advantage:	1.40%
Usefulness:	Very useful

Chapter Summary

The game is played primarily around the line bets—pass and don't pass. Each bet gives the house approximately a 1.4% advantage. Line bets can be backed up with a free odds wager that affords the house no advantage. When single odds are played, the overall house advantage drops to .8%; when double odds are played they drop to .6%. The come bet and the don't come bet are played identically to how the line bets are played with the only difference being that they are made after the come out roll, in effect establishing a players own "private" point. Players can make as many come and don't come bets as they like and all these bets can be backed with free odds in the same way as the line bets.

CHAPTER FOUR

Other Bets on the Layout

The bets previously outlined will serve as cornerstones of our winning strategies. There are many other bets available but only a very few of them will be useful to us. We will explain other wagers now and earmark those few useful ones.

The Field Bet

On each end of the table you'll find the relatively large and prominent section labeled "Field" which seems to have an abundance of winning numbers shown. One number is shown to "Pay Double" while another is shown to "Pay Triple." The field bet sometimes gets a lot of play, certainly more than it deserves. To the untrained eye it appears attractive and it certainly is easy enough to understand. If you ask the dealer how the bet works he'll explain that it's quite simple—the field bet is a one-roll bet that must be played for at least the table minimum. If any of the numbers shown in the box appear on the next roll, the wager wins at even money. Moreover, if the 2 is thrown the bet pays double and if the 12 is thrown the bet pays triple (depending on the casino, the 2 may pay triple and the 12 double). If any other number shows, the bet loses.

With so many numbers shown in the box and with the 2 and 12 having increased payoffs this bet looks like a bonanza! But don't give up your day job just yet. Let's examine the field using the statistics we now know about dice.

The field bet shows the winning numbers as 2, 3, 4, 9, 10, 11 and 12 while the losing numbers are 5, 6, 7, and 8. Clearly there are more winning numbers than losing numbers. However, the number of winning numbers versus losing numbers is not what matters. What matters is the number of winning combinations versus the number of losing combinations. Let's refer back to our dice chart on page 11. When we apply this to the field bet, the numbers shake out as follows:

Winning Number	Ways to Make	Vs.	Losing Numbers	Ways to Make
2	1		5	4
3	2		6	5
4	3		7	6
9	4		8	5
10	3			
11	2			
12	1			
Totals 7	16		4	20

As you can see, there are 7 winning numbers and only 4 losing numbers. However, as you can also see, there are only 16 combinations that make those winning numbers while 20 combinations make the losers!

To properly compare win-loss ratios we must add one combination for the 2 that pays double and two combinations for the 12 that pays triple. This accurately brings the win-loss ratio to 19 ways to win versus 20 ways to lose—a house advantage of 2.77%. Because this bet pushes the limit of how much advantage we ever want to give the house, we will incorporate it into our strategies in an extremely limited way.

On some craps layouts the 2 and 12 both pay only double, at which point the house advantage almost doubles to 5.26%. This renders the bet completely useless, and one that should never be made.

Field Bet
Summary
One Roll Bet
Placed by: The Player

3, 4, 9, 10 and 11:	Pays Even Money
2:	Pays Double
12:	Pays Triple
5, 6, 7 and 8:	Loses
Special Rules:	Must be made at or above table minimum. Always working.
House Advantage:	2.77% (if 2 or 12 pays triple)
Usefulness:	Very Limited

The Place Bets

The place bets are extremely popular because they offer fast action. Most gamblers are impatient by nature. Action on place bets requires virtually no waiting time. As we are about to learn, place bettors pay dearly for their impatience by consistently making these very popular bets.

You'll notice that the place numbers, 4, 5, 6, 8, 9, and 10, are all the potential point and come numbers. Rather than going through the come box and essentially letting the dice pick the numbers for you, you can "go" directly to a number, after the come out roll by making a place bet. Let's say, for example, that you want to bet that the 9 will come before the 7. You would simply put your chips, in multiples of $5's, in the come box and tell the dealer to "place the 9." The dealer will take the wager and put it in the box numbered 9. Depending on where you're standing at the table, he'll place the bet in a corresponding place in the box to designate it as your bet. At this point the bet is similar to a come bet with the point established as 9. If the 9 comes before the 7, you'll win at 7 to 5. If the 7 comes before the 9, you'll lose. All other numbers are neutral. If you make a $5 bet, you win $7. A $10 bet wins $14. A $500 bet wins $700 and so on.

How good a bet is this? If you'll recall there are 4 ways to make a 9: 6-3, 3-6, 5-4, 4-5. These would be winning rolls. There are 6 ways to make the seven: 6-1, 1-6, 2-5, 5-2, 4-3, 3-4, all losing rolls. The correct odds of a 9 coming before a seven are 4-6 or 2-3. The house pays 5-7, which of course is less than 2-3. This difference is the houses' edge, which calculates to a 4.00% advantage, which is a little stiff to beat. Below is a chart for all numbers made as place bets, with their payoffs versus correct odds and the resultant house advantage:

Number	Correct Odds	House Payoffs	House Advantages
4	2-1	9-5	6.67%
5	3-2	7-5	4.00%
6	6-5	7-6	1.52%
8	6-5	7-6	1.52%
9	3-2	7-5	4.00%
10	2-1	9-5	6.67%

As you can see, the house maintains a pretty substantial advantage over the place bettor, especially on the outside numbers. All these same numbers can be covered through the pass line or come box, and when played with odds will give the house less than a 1% advantage. The difference is that the place bettor can select the number and go directly to that number without waiting, whereas the come bettor allows the dice to select numbers. The premium the place bettor pays for instant action will prove to be substantial and unbeatable over time.

Sometimes place bettors place all numbers for maximum action. As a consistent come bettor (and winner) I frequently hear the same argument made by place bettors. Once they've placed their bets and, let's say, the 5 is thrown, they'll crow "See? My 5 won! Your come bet is just now going to the 5 and you need another 5 to win." This makes a weak case for place betting. First of all, the dice won't run out of 5s, or any number for that matter. Throwing one 5 does not diminish the probability of throwing another. I could also retort that if the 7 were thrown, which is a more likely occurrence than the 5 being thrown, I would have won my come bet (as I would with an 11), where he would have lost all his place bets! And my odds bet will pay correct odds of 3-2, not 7-5 as the 5 pays for the place bettor.

All the verbal argument in the world can't compete with the quantifiable statistics—the 5 as a place bet give the house a 4.00% advantage, while the come bet gives the house .8% with single odds or .6% with double odds. We want to discourage consistent action on place betting. Believe me, this is the wager the casino wants you to make.

Before we leave the subject, consider one more scenario. As mentioned above, you must bet in increments of $5 on the 4 and 10 and the 5 and 9 to receive the proper 9 to 5 and 7 to 5 payoffs, respectively (for the 6 and 8, to receive the 7-6 payoff you must bet in increments of $6). To cover all six winning numbers, the five dollar bettor would need $32. Let's suppose that he placed the six bets, and then the dice rolled the following sequence: 4, 9, 8 and 5—all winning numbers for our aggressive place bettor. On the 4 he would win $9; on the 9 he'd win $7; on the 8 he'd win $7; and on the 5 he'd win $7. His total winnings for those four rolls would be $30. If the fifth roll were a 7 he would lose $32, for a net loss of $2! The place bettor has to generally hit 5 or 6 numbers consecutively before a 7 appears, in order to make any kind of profit! Intuitively, one should realize this is not the way to play the game.

Finally, place bets are "off" on come out rolls unless otherwise requested. Place bets can be raised, lowered, taken down, left up, or called "off" at any time by the player.

Place Bets
Summary

Multiple roll bet

Placed by: The dealer

Placed number comes before 7:	Wins
	6, 8 pays 7 to 6
	5, 9 pays 7 to 5
	4, 10 pays 9 to 5
7 comes before Placed number:	Loses
All other numbers:	Neutral
Special rules:	Place bets are "off" on the come out roll but can be "on" if requested by the player. Must be made in increments that allow correct payoffs for maximum return. Must be made at or above table minimum.
House advantages:	6, 8–1.52%
	5, 9–4.00%
	4, 10–6.67%
Usefulness:	6 and 8–Some usefulness
	4, 5, 9, and 10–None

The Big Six and Big Eight

On each end of the layout, usually adjacent to the field bet, are the big six/big eight bets. The big six/big eight bets do not get much play. In fact, recently I've noticed more and more casinos are eliminating them from the table layout. No big loss. These bets give the house a huge 9.09% advantage. The big six and big eight are two separate bets that can be made one at a time or together, however the payoffs have no impact on each other. To bet the big six you merely place your chips in the designated box. To win, the 6 must come before the 7, in which case the bet pays even money. If the 7 comes first you lose. All other numbers are neutral.

If you see anyone make this bet, and you will from time to time, you'll instantly know this person has virtually no knowledge of craps. Clearly, if someone wanted to bet on the 6 coming before the 7 they could simply bet in increments of $6 on the 6 as a place bet and enjoy a 7 to 6 payoff while giving up only a 1.52% advantage! As you've probably already figured out, the big eight is the same bet except you are betting the 8 will come before the 7 for even money. Again, this gives the house a 9.09% advantage, and again, the same bet is available as a place bet on the 8 in increments of $6, for a 7 to 6 payoff and a house advantage of only 1.52%.

One minor difference worth noting between the big six/big eight and the 6 and 8 as place bets is that the big six/big eight are always working whereas the place bets are "off" on the come out roll, unless requested to be on.

Big Six & Big Eight
Bet Summary
Multiple Roll Bet
Placed by: The Player

6 (or 8) before 7:	Pays even money
7 before 6 (or 8):	Loses
All other numbers:	Neutral
Special rules:	6 and 8 bets have no effect on one another. Must be made at or above table minimum. Always working. Can be taken down at any time.
House advantage:	9.09%
Usefulness:	None

Buying the 4 and/or the 10

To encourage more place-like betting, the house allows the player to "buy" the 4 and/or the 10. This effectively reduces the house edge from 6.67% to 4.76%. To do this you must pay the house a 5% commission, or "vig" (short for "vigorish") as it is

sometimes called. If you buy the 4, the house will pay the correct odds of 2 to 1 should this bet win, instead of the place bet
payoff of 9 to 5. For example, if you wanted to bet $20 that the
4 will come before the 7, you could "buy" the 4. 5% of $20 is
$1 so you would give the dealer an extra dollar as the commis-
sion for booking the bet, which the house will retain whether
the bet is won or lost. The dealer will then place a "buy" button
on the bet to designate it as a "buy" bet to be paid off at 2-1
should it win. If after a few rolls the bet neither wins nor loses,
you can take the bet down at which time the commission will
be returned to you.

An important point is that the casino will not deal with
change on this bet. For example, if you wanted to bet $25 on
the 10, the commission at 5% would be $1.25 (5% of $25 =
$1.25) The casino will not take $1.25, but frequently they will
allow $25 to be bet for a $1.00 commission. They may even
allow $30 or $35 to be bet at the 2 to 1 payoff for only a $1.00
commission, and not until you bet the next level, say $40, will
they then charge $2.00 (5% of $40 = $2.00). It is much smarter
to bet $35 for $1 commission than $40 at $2.00. If you must
make this type of bet, ask the dealer what the maximum bet
level is (for your size betting) before the next higher commission kicks in. If $35 can be bet for $1, this reduces the house
advantage to close to 3%, not very good but better than 4.76%
and certainly better than 6.67% as a place bet. Nonetheless, this
bet should not be made.

Buying the 4 and/or 10
Bet Summary
Multiple Roll Bet
Placed by: The Dealer

4 (or 10) before 7:	Wins 2 to 1 (correct odds)
7 before 4 (or 10):	Loses
All other numbers:	neutral
Special rules:	Requires 5% commission. Bet can be taken down anytime (commission will be returned). Bet is "off" on come out rolls.
House Advantage:	4.76% (can be reduced)
Usefulness:	None

Lay Wagers

The casino also allows you to lay wagers against the point numbers; that is, to bet that the seven will come before either the 4, 5, 6, 8, 9, or 10. To do this you must "lay" money at the correct odds against the point number and pay a 5% commission, or "vig," on the potential winnings. Let's review our table of odds again as it relates to lay wagers.

Point Number	Ways to Make	Vs.	Ways to Make a Seven	Correct Odds	Casino Payoff	House Advantage After 5% Commission
4	3		6	1-2	1-2	2.44%
5	4		6	2-3	2-3	3.23%
6	5		6	5-6	5-6	4.00%
8	5		6	5-6	5-6	4.00%
9	4		6	2-3	2-3	3.23%
10	3		6	1-2	1-2	2.44%

Keep in mind, lay wagers are rarely made. We will find some limited usefulness with the 4 and 10 but the inside numbers give the house too great an edge and, consequently, are of no use. To make this bet you simply set your chips in the come box and verbally indicate to the dealer that you would like to lay odds against a particular point number. If you were to bet, let's say, $40 against the 4, then you would set down $40 plus an additional $1 chip as the 5% commission on the potential winnings should the 7 come before the 4. You might call out "lay wager against the four!" or simply "No four!" and the dealer will book the bet by placing the chips atop the appropriate place number and placing a "Lay" button on top of the chips. If you were betting against the 5 you might lay $30 to win $20, as the odds against the 5 are 2 to 3. The commission would again be $1 (5% of the potential winnings of $20.00). Similarly, a larger bettor might lay $600 to win $500 against the 6. The commission would then be 5% of $500, or $25.

As I mentioned, only the 4 and 10 will prove to be of value in this type of bet, and limited value at that. On these two numbers you can reduce the standard house edge of 2.44% in a way similar to how we reduced the house advantage on the 4 and 10 when we bought them.

For example we could, following the scenario above, lay $40 to win $20, which requires a commission of $1. However, if we wanted to lay $50 to win $25, the 5% commission would be $1.25. Again, the casino will not deal with change so they will round down in your favor. $50 bet to win $25 with a $1 commission calculates to a house advantage of 2%. You will have to ask the dealer how much can be laid against the number while still paying only $1 commission. Casinos vary on this.

If you're going to lay wagers, only do it on the 4 and 10. Limit the frequency of this bet and bet near the casino maximum for the minimum commission. This will tighten the hold on the casino advantage and will pay dividends over the long term. Remember, the house collects the commission whether the bet is won or lost. If after a win or loss you want to make the bet again, the commission must be paid again. The bet is always working and can be taken down at any time by the player, at which time the commission will be returned.

Lay Wagers
Bet Summary
Multiple Roll Bet
Placed by: The dealer

7 comes before number laid:	Wins at correct odds (less 5% commission)
Laid number comes before 7:	Loses
All other numbers:	Neutral
Special Rules:	Always working. Requires 5% commission. Can be taken down at anytime (commission will be returned if bet is taken down)
House Advantages:	6 and 8–4.00% 5 and 9–3.23% 4 and 10–2.44%(can be reduced)
Usefulness:	4 and 10–Limited 5,6,8, or 9–None

Proposition Bets

Proposition bets are those bets located in the center section of the table. They are under the direct control of the stickman. Proposition bets can be made below the table minimum. To make one of the many proposition bets you simply toss your chips (literally) to the middle of the table and call out your bet. The stickman will quickly collect up the chips and place them in the appropriate betting area.

A word about proposition bets: when I see a player tossing chips around and calling out proposition bets with any regularity I know immediately he is not a professional and definitely not a winner at this game. I know this because proposition bets give the house large advantages over the player—sometimes outrageously large advantages, as much as 16.67%. The proposition bettor may have a story or two about how years ago he

made a few thousand dollars one night at the table, but believe
me, it doesn't take much time for these odds to catch up with
you and quickly suck you down.

We hesitate to even cover proposition bets, as there is virtually no reason to ever use them. I say "virtually" because we
will use a couple of proposition bets to tip the dealers. We'll
learn exactly how and why in Chapter 11. Basically, though,
proposition bets are by far the worst bets the table has to offer,
despite their seemingly exotic and exciting nature and the temp-
tation of a high payoff. In the interest of making sure that anyone who reads this book will become well-versed in the entire
game—good bets and bad—we will cover all center bets here.

The Hardways

The hardways get a lot of action. They're usually located at the
top of the proposition bets in front of the boxman. When making a hardway bet you're betting that the particular number (4,
6, 8, or 10) will be made the "hard way" before it is made easy
or before a 7 is thrown. A number is said to be made hard when
the dice show a pair. For example, six is made the hardway
when the dice show a pair of threes (3-3) as opposed to being
made easy: 5-1, 1-5, 2-4 or 4-2. As the name implies, it is hard
to make the 6 as a pair of threes as there is only one way it can
happen, with each die showing its 3. This is only a 1 in 36 probability. However, as mentioned, the bet is that it will show hard
before it shows "easy" or before any 7 shows. Let's examine the
probability of this occurring versus the casino payoff. Of all 36
possible combinations only one, the 3-3, will win, while 10
combinations will lose. The losing numbers are the "easy" six
combinations (5-1, 1-5, 2-4, 4-2) and all six of the combinations
that make the 7 (6-1, 1-6, 5-2, 2-5, 3-4, 4-3). All other numbers
are neutral. The odds of winning are therefore 10 to 1. The
casino pays only 9 to 1 should the hard six show first, for a
house advantage of 9.09%. The following table shows all the

No.	Hard Way Winners	Easy Way Losers	Sevens Losers	Total No. of Losers	Correct Odds	House Edge Payoff	%
6	3,3	5-1, 1-5, 4-2, 2-4	6-1, 1-6, 5-2, 2-5, 4-3, 3-4	10	10-1	9-1	9.09
8	4,4	6-2, 2-6, 5-3, 3-5	6-1, 1-6, 5-2, 2-5, 4-3, 3-4	10	10-1	9-1	9.09
4	2,2	3-1, 1-3	6-1, 1-6, 5-2, 2-5, 4-3, 3-4	8	8-1	7-1	11.1
10	5,5	6-4, 4-6	6-1, 1-6, 5-2, 2-5, 4-3, 3-4	8	8-1	7-1	11.1

hardway numbers, their losers, the correct odds, the house pay-offs and the resultant house edge:

As you can see in the house edge column, the house maintains an excessive advantage on hardway bets. Don't be lured into playing these poor bets by the high payoffs or by the hawking of the stickman. The percentage on these wagers prohibits them from being of any use in a winning strategy.

Hardway
Bet Summary
Multiple Roll Bet
Placed by: The Stickman

4, 6, 8, or 10 (whichever bet on) made hard:	Wins (see above chart)
Any 7 or 4, 6, 8 or 10 (whichever bet on) made easy:	Loses
Special rules:	Always working. May be made below table minimum. May be taken down at any time.
House Advantage:	Hard 6 or 8–9.09% Hard 4 or 10–11.1%
Usefulness:	None (Except for tipping)

Any Seven

The any seven bet is as simple as it is bad. You're betting that the next roll of the dice will be a 7 in any combination. If the next roll is a 7, you win at 4 to 1. If any other number shows, you lose.

Let's take a quick look at this proposition. There are 36 possible combinations the dice can make. Six of them will win while thirty of them will lose. 6 versus 30 reduces down to 5 to 1. The casino only pays 4 to 1 on this probability. This calculates to an obscene 16.67% house advantage. This means you can expect to lose $16.67 for every $100 bet on the any 7! If you remember our coin-tossing friend in Chapter 3, we were only giving him a 5% advantage—and he was our friend! You can either give the casino what they want or save your money for a good show.

Any Seven
Bet Summary
One Roll Bet
Placed by: The Stickman

Any 7:	Wins at 4 to 1
All other numbers:	Lose
Special Rules:	Always working. Can be made below table minimum
House Advantage:	16.67%
Usefulness:	None

Any Craps

Any craps proposes that the next roll of the dice will be either a 2, 3 or 12. Any of these numbers will pay off at 7 to 1. But wait a minute! What are the real odds of this occurring? There are 4 possible combinations that will win. One for the 2, two for the 3, and one for the 12, for a total of 4. This leaves 32 possible losing combinations. 32 to 4 reduces down to 8 to 1. Our casino pays only 7 to 1, leaving an advantage to the house of 11.1%, which is far above the professional player's tolerance.

Despite the large house advantage, this bet gets a lot of play, especially on the come out roll. Players reason this is a good "hedge" on their pass line bet, meaning that if they crap out they'll lose their line bet but at least they'll even out with an any craps bet.

Remember one thing. This is a game steeped in statistics, not one of intuitive reason. We cannot take a bet of nominal loss expectation (a pass line bet) and combine it with a bet of high loss expectation (any craps) and produce a positive outcome. Stick with statistical correctness. This is the first step of professional play.

Any Craps
Bet Summary
One Roll Bet
Placed by: The Stickman
2, 3 or 12 (Any Craps): Wins at 7 to 1
All other numbers: Lose
Special rules: Always working. Can be made below
table minimum
House advantage: 11.1%
Usefulness: None

Betting the 2, 3, 11 or 12

These are all one-roll bets, made individually and placed by the
stickman. You're simply betting that the next roll of the dice
will be the number bet on. Any other number loses. The following chart will best illustrate the house advantages on each
of these silly bets:

Number	Ways to Make	Ways to Lose	Odds Reduced Down	Casino Payoff	House Advantage
2	1	35	35 to 1	30 to 1*	13.89%
3	2	34	17 to 1	15 to 1**	11.1%
11	2	34	17 to 1	15 to 1**	11.1%
12	1	35	35 to 1	30 to 1*	13.89%

** Sometimes pays 15 for 1 or 14 to 1 (same thing)—House Advantage 16.67%
* Sometimes pays 30 for 1 or 29 to 1 (same thing)—House Advantage 16.67%

These bets, with their ridiculous house advantages, do nothing more than pay the salaries of the casino personnel. Let some
one else pay them!

Betting the 2, 3, 11, or 12
Bet Summary
One Roll Bet
Placed by: The stickman

Number bet on (2, 3, 11, or 12):	Wins (see above chart)
All other numbers:	Lose
Special Rules:	Always working. May be made below table minimum.
House advantage:	(See above chart)
Usefulness:	None

The Horn Bet

The horn bet is unique because it allows you to make four very bad bets all at once. Here, you're betting on the 2, 3, 11, and 12 all at the same time while covering them all individually. Consequently, you must make bets equally divisible by 4. For example, if you toss $20 to the stickman and call out "around the horn!" he will break this down to four $5 bets on each of the numbers 2, 3, 11 and 12. If one of these numbers show on the next roll you'll win at the usual poor casino payoff, but at the same time you necessarily lose the other three bets! That is to say, if you collect on one number the other three numbers must lose! And this would be the best outcome you could hope for. You could lose all four! Let's return to our example. We bet $20 "around the horn". That is, $5 on each of the four numbers 2, 3, 11, and 12. If the 12 is thrown we would win $150 (30-1) plus the return of the $5 bet covering the 12. The other three bets of $5 each would lose totaling $15. Therefore only $140 would be returned. If the 3 were thrown we would win $75 (15-1) plus the return of our $5 covering the 3. We would lose $15 on the other 3 bets for a net returned to us of $65 for our $20 bet. If a non-horn number is thrown, we lose all four bets totaling $20.00. The horn bet is sheer foolishness and should not be made.

Horn Bet
Summary
One Roll Bet
Placed by: The Stickman
2, 3, 11, or 12: Wins (other 3 numbers will lose)
4, 5, 6, 7, 8, 9, and 10: Lose
Special rules: May be made below table minimum.
Always working. Bet is divided by four to
cover all four numbers, if one number
wins the other 3 numbers necessarily
lose.
House advantage: 2 or 12 at 29-1, 16.67%
2 or 12 at 30-1, 13.89%
3 or 11 at 15-1, 11.1%
3 or 11 at 14-1, 16.67%
Usefulness: None

The Hop Bet

From time to time you'll hear a player make what is called a hop
bet or bet a number "on the hop". There is no nomenclature on
the layout referring to this bet but it is available in almost all
casinos. This bet is unique because it is the only bet that is given
to the boxman as opposed to one of the standing dealers or the
stickman or making the bet yourself. The hop bet is a one-roll
bet where the player is betting on not only the total of the roll,
but also exactly which numbers the dice will show individually.

If the number bet on is a pair, for example a 5-5, and on the
next roll the pair shows, the casino will payoff at 29 to 1 or 30
to 1, depending on the house rule. Any other result will lose.
Of course, the true odds of one particular pair showing are 35
to 1. If the casino pays off at 30 to 1, they hold an advantage
of 13.29%. If it pays 29 to 1 the advantage is 16.67%. For numbers 4 through 10 (excluding hardways) this is sometimes called
"on the turn".

If the number bet on is not a pair, say 5-4 for example
(thereby being 2 possible winning combinations), and that

combination shows on the next roll, then the casino will pay 15 to 1 or 14 to 1, whatever their standard is. Any other number loses. The true odds of any designated non-pair showing on one roll is 17 to 1, leaving the house an advantage of 11.1% when paid at 15 to 1 and an obscene 16.67% when paid at 14 to 1. Whatever the casino pays, you're advised to never engage in this grossly disadvantageous bet.

Hop Bet
Summary
One Roll Bet
Placed by: The boxman
Specific combination bet on
(pair or non-pair): Wins
All other numbers: Lose

House Advantage: Pairs paid at 30 to 1—13.89%
Pairs paid at 29 to 1—16.67%
Non-pairs paid at 15 to 1—11.1%
Non-pairs paid at 14 to 1—16.67%
Usefulness: None

"No Call Bets"

On most layouts you will see the words "No Call Bets" imprinted. Years ago, casinos regularly faced a scam where a player who had no money on him would walk up to a table when the dice were in the air and call out a bet. If the bet won, he would collect his winnings and leave. For example, he could walk up to a table as the dice flew and call out "Fifty on the field!". If one of the field numbers showed, he would collect his $50. If the two or twelve appeared, it was dinner that night at the finest steak house in town with a payoff of either $100 or $150. With no money to back the bet, these were the best odds anywhere! If, however, the bet lost, the casino would want their money which, of course, the player did not have. You can't squeeze blood from a turnip, so the only option would be to throw the "patron" out on his ear. For those who could take the abuse that came after losses, a nice chunk of change could be made walking the strip this way. The casinos now want both the unscrupulous and the dealers to be well advised that no call bets will be accepted.

In the more modern day application, the house simply wants to be sure that as a player nears the bottom of his stake, he doesn't carelessly call out a bet he cannot cover. If, in fact, a player has plenty of money in front of him and the dice are in the air, he might call out "odds on my four!" or "$10 on the come!". At this point the dealer would probably book the bet by audibly confirming the bet is on. As soon as the dice land, the appropriate chips should change hands.

"To" One versus "For" One

On some craps layouts you'll see the payoffs on the proposition bets quoted as "to" one, as in "9 to 1," while on other layouts the same bet will be quoted as "for" one, as in "10 for 1." I don't want anyone to be confused or mislead by this difference. When a payoff is quoted at "for" one, it means the payoff includes the original bet with it. If the payoff is quoted as "to" one, they are simply breaking apart the payoff from the original bet—which is how payoffs and odds are usually quoted.

A payoff of 9 to 1 is the same as a payoff quoted at 10 for 1. 10 "for" 1 means if the bet wins you'll receive 10 times the original bet back, which includes the original amount bet. If one dollar is bet you'd receive $10 back; $9 in winnings plus the original $1 bet—10 for 1. When quoted at 9 to 1, you'll receive the same thing, $9 in winnings plus $1 for the bet. If you walk up to a table and see the hard six and eight quoted at 10 for 1, you'll know this is not an advantage over the casinos that quotes the payoffs as 9 to 1. If you hear the boxman quote a hop bet payoff as 30 for 1, you'll know the payoff is really 29 to 1. If he said 30 to 1 that would be slightly better for the player.

Chapter Summary

Of all the bets covered in this chapter, only the field bet, lay wagers on the 4 & 10, and place bets on the 6 & 8 are of any use at all, and limited at that.

Propositions bets, with their obscenely high house advantages ranging from 9.09% to 16.67%, have no place in long-term winning or professional play (except for the hardway bets for tipping). This is where, percentage-wise, the dice pits make most of their money. There is no way a player can overcome these disadvantages over any long-term time frame.

If, by some quirk of fate, all players suddenly refrained from making proposition bets, betting the big 6 and big 8, field bets, and place numbers, and everyone consistently made only line bets with maximum odds, the casinos might very well close up their dice tables. A .6% house advantage would not pay the salaries and other expenses incurred in running the games. Now, we wouldn't want that to happen—we'd have nowhere to play! So to all those uninformed, thrill-seeking players out there . . . keep those chips a-flying!

CHAPTER FIVE

Understanding Streaks

Streaks are very much a part of gambling. Understanding the nature of streaks and coming to grips with the damage they can cause if miss-managed, as well as the profits they can bring if managed properly, is a key to any winning strategy.

We'll define a streak, for gaming purposes, as an event with a roughly 50% chance of occurring doing so 2 or more times in immediate succession. If one flips a coin ten times and the result is alternating heads and tails then it could be said a streak did not occur.

It has been my experience that most people believe if an event with a roughly 50% chance of occurring has occurred, say, 3 or 4 times in a row, then the opposite event becomes more likely to occur. Nothing could be further from the truth nor more potentially damaging to the gambler. Even after 3 or 4 in a row, both possibilities remain with their approximate 50% probabilities firmly intact.

Perhaps the most convincing way to explain why managing streaks is critical to successful gaming over the long term is by example or, more accurately, by bad example—by showing how streaks can be mismanaged with devastating results.

Let's consider the classic "Martingale" system of betting. For the sake of simplicity, let's bet at the roulette table either red or black; an approximate 50-50 proposition. The Martingale is perhaps the best known system of betting and has been around for literally centuries. The system adopted its name from a London casino proprietor in the early eighteenth century. He would encourage his patrons to "double up" on their losses to enable them to catch up quickly. Essentially this only encourages more money to be bet on the table, which is exactly the casino's aim, and ultimately translates into casino profits.

To this day many people still believe this is a foolproof way to win. Some believe it is so effective that some casinos and even some states have outlawed this method of play. Let's see why this is not only a faulty system, but also one the casino will actually invite you to use. The Martingale system provides that one select a minimum bet and continue to bet that minimum until a loss occurs. Upon losing you simply double the bet. If a second loss occurs you double again and continue to double the bet until a win occurs at which point the net result to the bettor is plus one unit. Theoretically one could lose, say, four times in a row, then win once and be ahead. One could reason that he lost 80% of his bets and won only 20% of his bets and still made money. That is to say, he won money without beating the odds!! Therein lies the illusion.

If the minimum bet is $10 then upon a loss you would bet $20. If a second loss occurred you would bet $40, upon a third loss you would bet $80, and so on. As soon as a win occurred you would have a net result of plus $10. Essentially this system allows you to sustain more losses than wins and still make money! "The mother lode!" you say? Let's carry this system out a little further.

If you started at the table with a bet of $10, upon 9 successive wins you would have a profit of $90. However, consider the following chart that illustrates the progression of bets upon a losing streak:

	Required Bet	Total Money Bet
Initial Bet	$10	$10
1st Loss	$20	$30
2nd Loss	$40	$70
3rd Loss	$80	$150
4th Loss	$160	$310
5th Loss	$320	$630
6th Loss	$640	$1,270
7th Loss	$1,280	$2,550
8th Loss	$2,560	$5,110
9th Loss	$5,120	$10,230

As you can see, after your 5th loss you would be down $630 and would need to bet $640. If you won you would be plus $10 for all your efforts. However if you lost you would now be required to bet $1,280, facing current losses thus far of $1,270. At this point it is particularly relevant to point out that a win is not more likely now than on your first bet. The odds remain unchanged. Further, to get this far you would have had to come to the table with $2,560 and make an initial $10 bet; certainly possible but not realistic.

If one were to run this program on a computer it would prove to be an unbeatable system. Ultimately, when a win does occur, the player will be plus $10. But in the real world one generally does not have unlimited funds to bring to the table nor does one have unlimited nerve. Now, the odds of losing 9 times in a row on a near 50-50 proposition are approximately 512 to 1. To sustain 9 losses in a row, our $10 bettor would have to bring to the table for each gaming session $10,230 and make an initial bet of $10!

To be sure, one can play the Martingale system on any number of gaming sessions and walk away with modest wins each time. But, if your bet progression or policy is to double up on losses every time then there will be eventual catastrophic loses occurring that will more than wipe out any succession of modest gains—guaranteed.

I have never heard of any professional gambler who has shown a profit by the Martingale system or any similar system, and I'm certain I never will. As any credible gaming authority will advise, you must only increase bets when winning—never when losing! The forgoing is a classic example of how, if losing streaks are mismanaged, tremendous damage can occur. Losing streaks must be managed as to let them run their course with minimum damage to the bankroll while systematically increasing bets on winning streaks to yield maximum profits.

Two Contradictory Truths

1) You can't predict what the dice will do next
2) If you are alert to the dice you can learn to capitalize on streaks

These two statements contradict each other, yet both are true. While this may seem to defy logic, understanding both concepts is a key to winning. If played correctly, a streak of just 3 or 4 passes in a row will net you a beautiful win. But if the dice pass twice, is this the start of a streak? Can you be certain they'll pass again? Of course not. The fact is, we are not trying to predict what the dice will do—that is impossible (see truth #1). What is possible is to learn policies and bet progressions to best handle streaks—both winning and losing—when they do occur (see truth #2).

I remember playing once at the M.G.M. Grand in Las Vegas. There were six dice tables open on a Friday night. Four were groaning in agony while the two other were quite rowdy, one particularly so. I generally play pass line, but that night I wanted to play a "don't" game. Where would you start a "don't" game? Would you try to fight a trend at a hot table in hopes of catching the "turning" point? Or would you go with the flow? I was alerted to one table by the stickman's words "Out! Seven out. Line away," followed by the collective groan of the 5 remaining players at the table. I cashed in immediately. Did I know for certain this table would stay cold? Certainly not. I made about 50% of my bankroll in 20 minutes and walked away a winner. Now, it's true the table next to us was yelling, screaming, and slapping high fives as if they just won the Super Bowl. While this was quite annoying, a win is a win. And so it goes.

Certainly dice, like any other game of chance, does not run in predictable patterns of extended streaks. But the big money is made and lost based on how these streaks are managed when they do occur. And the best teacher of the nature of streaks is experience. You should gain this experience in the privacy and comfort of your own home, not at the casino in live play with real money.

So, no, casinos will not bar players who systematically double up on losses. Casinos will happily allow you to double up on losses—they will even serve you drinks and smile at you while you do it.

Chapter Summary

Essentially, what is being said here is that streaks are very much an integral part of gambling and that streak management is key to any winning strategy. To be sure, no one can predict what the dice will do, but any credible gaming expert will advise to only increase bets when winning—never when losing. This will minimize damage when losing steaks do occur while maximizing gains when winning streaks are at hand.

CHAPTER SIX

Bet Patterns

Now, armed with the knowledge of exactly how all the various wagers work, and of the corresponding advantages the house enjoys on each of them, we will analyze the best combinations to minimize exposure to excessive risk while capitalizing on winning streaks. We call these bet patterns. We will discuss bet patterns for the right bettor as well as the wrong bettor, both conservative and aggressive strategies.

Craps players should learn both sides of the dice well, meaning both pass and don't Pass, in order to be flexible enough to take advantage of trends as they occur. Further, intimately knowing both sides of play helps the player to understand the peaks and valleys and to deal with them, both financially and emotionally.

The bet pattern or patterns you choose to play ultimately will reflect a number of factors. Your knowledge of the game, your bankroll, your personality and temperament, your risk tolerance, and your emotional state as you begin a gaming session, all come together to construct your bet pattern for a particular session. You'll better understand what this means as we progress through the final chapters.

The 3% Rule

Whatever patterns you choose, you should always give the house only a very small statistical edge. The rule of thumb is to never give the house more than a 3% advantage on any bet. We call this the 3% rule. Further, the closer to 3% the house advantage is, the less frequently the bet should be used. Consider the following chart of all wagers, their corresponding house advantages, and their recommended frequency of use:

3% Rule Chart

House Advantage	Bet	Recommended Frequency of Use
0%	Free odds (with Pass/Come Bets)	100%
0%	Free odds (with Don't Pass/Don't Come)	100%
1.41%	Pass Line	100%
1.40%	Don't Pass	100%
1.41%	Come	100%
1.40%	Don't Come	100%
1.52%	Place Bets 6 & 8	50%
2.44%*	Lay Wager on 4 or 10	25%
2.77%	Field (where 2 or 12 Pay Triple)	20%
3% 3%		
3.23%	Lay Wager (5 & 9)	0%
4.00%	Lay Wager (6 & 8)	0%
4.00%	Place Bet (5 &9)	0%
4.76%*	Buy Bet (4 & 10)	0%
5.26%	Field (Where 2 & 12 Pay Double)	0%
6.67%	Place Bet (4 & 10)	0%
9.09%	Big 6 & 8	0%
9.09%	**Hardways 6 & 8	0%
11.11%	**Hardways 4 & 10	0%
11.11%	**Any Craps	0%
11.11%	**Eleven (@ 15 to 1)	0%
11.11%	**Three (@ 15 to 1)	0%
13.89%	**Two (@ 30 to 1)	0%
13.89%	**Twelve (@ 30 to 1)	0%
13.89%	**Hop Bet (@ 30 to 1)	0%
16.67%	**Hop Bet (@ 29 to 1)	0%
16.67%	**Any Seven	0%

* Can be improved upon. See Section on lay wagers or Buying the 4 & 10.
** Proposition Bets (Center of Table)

As you can see, the majority of the bets available offer more than a 3% advantage to the house. Some bets, mainly the proposition bets with their alluringly high payoffs, give an obscene house advantage. For any one session the player should select a bet pattern based around one of the line bets, either pass line (right betting) or don't pass (wrong betting). The bet pattern should include either taking double odds or laying double odds, depending on which side the player has selected. The line bets should be kept in play 100% of the time along with taking or laying double odds. The pass line bettor might opt to incorporate come bets with double odds and, to a lesser extent, the 6 & 8 as place bets. The don't pass bettor might use don't come bets, laying double odds, and he also might lay wagers on the 4 & 10 and field bets, though to a lesser extent due to their higher house edges. We will now cover the recommended betting patterns for both the right and wrong bettor, both conservative and aggressive strategies.

Pass Line with 1 Come Bet
Both with Double Odds
(Right Side—Conservative)

This simple yet effective bet pattern calls for the player to make one pass line bet and then back it up with double odds once the point is established. After the point is established we immediately make one come bet and back it up with double odds. Now, with two numbers working for us we stop betting (bear in mind that when putting into play any of our bet patterns, rolls of craps and eleven are ignored whether betting right or wrong). At this point we stand ready to keep two numbers in play backed with full double odds at all times. That is to say, if either the pass line number or the come number repeats and is thereby won, we immediately replace it and follow up with double odds.

For example, if the come number repeats, we collect the winnings and make another come bet and back it with double odds. The pass line bet, of course, would be unaffected by this. Similarly, if the point were repeated, our pass line bet would be paid off. The disk would go "Off" and we would be coming out again for a new roll. Our come bet would have been unaffected by the point repeating and would remain up. At this point we would make another pass line bet in our effort to keep two numbers in play at all times. Remember once again that now, on the come out roll, we ignore rolls of craps and eleven when trying to establish our point. Further remember that our odds bet on our come number is not working on come out rolls. If the 7 is rolled the come number is lost while we win our line bet and the odds will be returned to us. Don't forget to pick them up.

This bet pattern is quite conservative for two reasons. First, the Player never has too much exposure or risk to the 7 as only 2 numbers are covered at any one time. Second, the player has locked the house advantage to a scant .6% or, if playing single odds, .8%. Double odds are always preferred.

Properly capitalized (we'll get into bank roll and money management in Chapter 8) one should be able to meet the house virtually head on, statistically speaking, and consequently play for a long time, offering a chance for a hot roll to develop. Should a few numbers repeat before a 7 you can easily double your money or better.

This is a simple, safe and sane way to approach any craps table. We strongly suggest to the beginner to play this rudimentary and statistically sound bet pattern for at least the first few times at live casino play.

Pass Line Bet with 2 Come Numbers
All with Double Odds
(Right Side—Aggressive)

To gain more action while keeping the house's edge at the bare minimum, we simply make 2 come bets, instead of one, after our pass line bet, and back each with double odds. With three numbers now covered we'll have a bit more money vulnerable to the 7, but should numbers start repeating, more money will be made in a brief period. Bear in mind, the casino's advantage still remains locked at .6% when double odds are played on all numbers.

To better illustrate this pattern in action let's walk through a typical run of the dice. (There really is no such thing as a "typical run of the dice," but let's suspend reality for a moment for illustrative purposes.) We will follow a $10 bettor taking double odds. The disk is "off" and the stickman calls "New shooter coming out."

We put $10 on the pass line, and the dice are rolled:

Come Out Roll	9 (point)	Bet $20 in double odds behind our Pass line bet. Bet $10 in the come box.
First Come Roll	6	Dealer moves our come bet to the 6. We throw $20 to the dealer indicating our double odds bet on the 6. Bet $10 again in the come box in an effort to establish a second come number.
Second Come Roll	5	Dealer moves our $10 come bet to the 5. We throw $20 to the dealer, indicating our double odds bet on the 5.

Now, our pass line bet with a point of 9 is established, as are two come bets, one on the 5 and one on the 6, all backed with double odds—and we stop betting. We now have $90 on the layout. If a come number repeats, we collect our winnings and immediately replace it with another come bet. When that come number is established we back it up with double odds. Similarly, if the pass line bet repeats we collect our winnings and make a new pass line bet, as we will be coming out again. Of course, if the 7 is thrown all is lost. Let's continue.

Next Come Roll	8	No effect on our bets.
Next Come Roll	3 (craps)	No effect on our bets.
Next Come Roll	5	$40 win on the 5 ($10 on the come bet Plus $30 on the odds bet at 3-2). The bet comes down and we return the chips to our rails. We again wager $10 In the come box.
Next Come Roll	11	$10 win on the come bet. We return winnings to rail and leave the $10 bet in the come box.
Next Come Roll	4	Dealer moves come bet to the 4. We bet $20 in odds on the 4.

(Again, we have our pass line bet and two come bets working, all with double odds, so we stop betting.)

Next Come Roll	10	No effect on our bets.
Next Come Roll	9	$40 win on point. ($10 on the pass line bet plus $30 on the odds bet at 3-2).

Now that the point has been made, let's pause again and assess our situation.

Our two come bets on the 4 and 6 both remain with double odds of $20 each. The disc goes "off" and we'll be coming out again for a new roll. With the come bets currently established we need only establish a pass line bet, so we put $10 on the pass line.

An important rule to remember: odds on come bets are not working on come out rolls. What this means is that the odds are off and regardless of what number is thrown on the come out roll the odds portion of the come bet can neither be won nor lost. The reason for this is rather simple. Many pass line players will play some come bets and back them up with odds. If a point is repeated then the table will be coming out again. At this point the pass line bettors will be hoping for the 7 for a win on their Line bet. But they also know that if the 7 comes they'll lose their existing come bets along with their odds! This would prompt most right side bettors to ask the dealers to take their odds bets down for the come out roll. Then, after a new point is established, they would want to reestablish all their odds bets. If there were a lot of right side bettors at the table, this kind of make-work program would drive the dealers crazy! So, it is standard procedure at all casinos that odds on come bets are off on come out rolls.

Now, you can't take the underlying come bet down because the house maintains an edge over the player on those bets and is not willing to relinquish that edge. The house holds no such advantage on the odds bet, so this is an easy rule for the house to incorporate into standard play. The player does have the option, however, of requesting that his odds remain working on the come out roll, at which point the dealer will set an "on" button on top of the player's odds. The player cannot tell the dealer that he will play the whole session with his odds working on come out rolls. He must specifically request it on each and every come out roll, or else the odds will automatically be off. Let's continue with our scenario:

Come Out Roll	2 (craps)	Lose $10 on pass line. Bet another $10 on the pass line.
Second Come Out Roll	10 (point)	We bet $20 in odds—behind the line.
1st Come Roll	12 (craps)	No effect on our bet.
2nd Come Roll	4	Win $50 on come bet of 4 ($10 on underlying bet plus $40 on the double odds bet at 2 to 1). Bet $10 in come box.
Next Come Roll	6	Win $34 on the existing come bet of 6 ($10 + $24). The new come bet moves to the 6. We

Next Come Roll   7

bet $20 in odds and another $10 in the come box.

Ouch!! Game over. Win $10 on the come bet (Don't forget to pick it up.) Lose $30 on pass line bet and $30 on our come bet on the 4.

Result:
Total Winning: $184
Total Losses: 70

NET WIN   +$114

So, in our hypothetical first game there were 16 rolls. We made one point and 3 come numbers. We won one 11 and lost on one craps. Our net win is $114.00. The layout is cleared, the disc goes "off," and we're ready to start again.

This bet pattern is aggressive and can yield a nice win without having too much at risk to the 7. To ratchet this pattern up one more notch in aggressiveness we could simply add another come bet. However, during a nice roll of the dice we prefer to incorporate place bets instead of more come bets, as delineated in the following preferred bet pattern.

Pass Line Bet with 2 Come Numbers All with Double Odds While Keeping the 6 and 8 Covered as Place Bets (Right Side—Most Aggressive)

This is the most aggressive of all right betting strategies. Here we're putting more money in play and we're giving the house a bit more advantage insofar as when the 6 and/or 8 are placed the house maintains a 1.52% advantage. With this pattern we are endeavoring to keep all inside numbers—the 5, 6, 8 and 9—covered, particularly the 6 and 8 as they are the cornerstones of most any hot roll. We start this aggressive pattern by first making our pass line bet and backing it up with double odds.

We then make two come bets, both with double odds. If, after establishing our three numbers, either the 6 or 8 has not been covered, we toss chips down (into the come box) and indicate to the dealer we are making place bets on either the 6, 8, or both, depending on what is not covered. The place bets should be made in size equal to the line bet including the double odds. For example: if we were betting $10 plus $20 in double odds for a total of $30, we would bet $30 on each of our place bets on the 6 and/or 8. At 7 to 6 these bets would pay $35 if won. If our bet size on the line is $50 plus $100 in double odds for a total of $150, then our place bet size might be $120 or $150 to win $140 or $175 respectively.

If we play this strategy correctly, our $10 bettor could have as many as 5 numbers covered for a total of $150 on the lay-out—all vulnerable to the 7. This pattern should be played only by experienced players who truly understand the volatility of the game as it relates to streaks.

Let's go through another run of the dice to illustrate this pattern. The disk is "off" and we're coming out. We put $10 on the pass line and the dice are thrown.

Come Out Roll	5 (point)	We bet $20 in double odds behind the line and $10 in the come box.
1st Come Roll	8	We bet $20 in odds on the 8 and bet $10 in the come box.
2nd Come Roll	3 (craps)	Lose $10 on the come bet. Replace it with $10.
Next Come Roll	10	Our come bet moves to the 10, we back it up with double odds.

Now, with our pass line and two come bets covering the 5 (point), 8 and 10, we see the 6 is not covered, so we bet $30 as a place bet on the 6. It's worth repeating again that you've now given the house a 1.52% advantage on this wager, but should the dice warm up you'll be in position to make a number of collections.

Anyway, we now have 4 numbers covered and we make no new wagers. Let's continue:

Next Come Roll	12 (craps)	No action for us.
Next Roll	10	Win $50 on the come bet ($10 plus $40 on odds at 2 to 1). Bet $10 in the come box.
Next Roll	11	Win $10 on come bet. Return winnings to rails. Leave $10 in come Box.
Next Roll	8	Win $34 on the come bet ($10 plus $24 in double odds at 6 to 5) The come bet moves to the 8. We bet $10 in the come box. Note: When the existing come bet is the same size as the bet in the come box the dealer will simply pay you the winnings, in this case $34, and leave the existing come bets untouched. This is called "off and on". Don't let it throw you. It's just a short cut to taking the existing come bet down, collecting your winnings, moving the new come bet up and then re-establishing the odds bet. Think about it.
Next Roll	6	Win $35 on our place bet. We now request the bet be taken down as our come bet will now move to the 6. We back the come bet with $20 in odds.

We now have the point of 5 and two come bets covering the 6 and 8. Now, with three numbers covered including the 6 & 8 we stop betting. Let's continue:

Next Roll	9	No action for us.
Next Roll	8	Win $34 on the come bet of 8 ($10 plus $24 in odds.) The bet comes down. Bet $10 in come box.
Next Roll	2 (craps)	Lose $10 on come bet. Replace $10 come bet.
Next Roll	10	Our come bet moves to the 10 and we back it up with double odds. Now, with the eight uncovered we immediately cover it with a $30 place bet.
Next Roll	5 (point)	Win $40 on the point ($10 plus $30).

We now have the 6 and 10 covered with come bets and the 8 covered as a place bet. The disc goes "off" and we're now coming out again. We bet $10 on the pass line:

Next Roll	7	"Out"

Remember, odds on come bets and place bets are off on come out rolls. Therefore, we lose $10 on each of our come bets on the 6 and 10 for a total of $20. Our odds are returned to us, and we win $10 on our pass line bet and our place bet on the 8 remains up. We would normally continue on this fairly warm roll but let's stop now and see where we stand. The dice were thrown a total of 15 times. We hit 3 come numbers, 1 point, 1 place bet, 1 eleven, lost on two craps and sevened out on a come roll (saving the odds and a place bet):

Result:

Total Win	$213
Total Losses	40
Net Win	$173

This bet pattern provides the most action, the most risk, and, consequently, the biggest upside potential should a hot roll develop.

Bet Patterns to Avoid

As our recommended bet patterns are based on statistical correctness, our patterns to avoid are based on statistical "incorrectness." You'll find many players make a pass line bet and then, rather than back it up with odds, they "use" the money to make place bets on all remaining numbers. This pattern yields mega-action (which is what most gamblers are looking for) as well as mega-losses. For the player who bets this way, the pass line without odds gives a 1.41% advantage away to the casino and we go downhill from there. The 6 & 8 placed give 1.52%, the 5 & 9 give 4.00% and the 4 & 10 a whopping 6.67%. The masochist, not content with these insurmountable odds, will play a few hardway bets at 9.09 or 11.1% or perhaps randomly throw out any craps or bet the eleven, each at 11.1%. These players might look and sound like experts or big-shots, they might have all the right moves and the hot vernacular, but you'll know better. Stick to statistical correctness and limit your exposure to risk. Along with proper money management and the progressions presented in the next few chapters, you'll put all the would-be big shots to shame.

Don't Pass (Wrong Side Betting)

As noted earlier, it is important to learn both sides of the dice—the right side and the wrong side. First, you should know how to play both sides in order to take advantage of streaks or trends as they occur. Second, knowing the angles will help you deal with the action both financially and emotionally. Remember, when we say "wrong" side betting we are referring to don't pass betting, which can be every bit as profitable as pass line betting. There is nothing "wrong" about that!

As we go over the recommended don't side strategies, you'll notice they're very similar to right side betting. Realizing this makes it all easier to understand.

Again, any bet pattern should be based on statistical correctness. We'll recommend 3 such patterns here—conservative, aggressive, and most aggressive—while never violating the 3% rule.

Don't Pass with 1 Don't Come Bet
Both Laying Double Odds
(Wrong Side—Conservative)

The subheading above sums it up. We make our line bet on the don't passline. Once the point has been established we lay full double odds against the point. We then make a don't come bet in an effort to establish one don't come number. Once the don't come number is established we lay double odds against that number. With our don't pass bet plus one don't come bet established, with full double odds laid against each, we stop betting. Now, unlike Right side betting where all is at risk to the 7, we can only lose one bet on any one roll should one of our numbers repeat. Should the 7 appear, we win both our bets.

With only two don't numbers established we have limited our exposure to two numbers that might repeat and be lost. We have also reduced the house advantage to .6% (.8% if we choose to lay only single odds).

Now, if the don't come number repeats and is thereby lost, we replace it with another don't come bet. Once the new don't come bet is reestablished we again lay double odds against it. It is extremely important to point out that we never replace the don't come bet more than one time. The reason for this is to protect against the hot roll where point numbers continually repeat thereby losing all don't come bets along with their full double odds.

Similarly, if the don't pass number (the point) repeats—a loser for us—we will then be coming out and trying another don't pass bet. If the point repeats again, thereby losing for us, we do not make another don't pass bet but rather we simply wait for the shooter to seven out on this moderately hot roll, and then we start again once he does. This is an important stop gap rule the don't bettor should always employ to protect against the hot roll.

For the conservative don't bettor this is a safe way to work the table and ensure a nice profit if the table turns cold, while at the same time limiting exposure to losses.

Don't Pass Betwith 2 Don't Come Bets
All with Double Odds Laid Against
(Wrong Side—Aggressive)

By merely adding one don't come bet we substantially increase the aggressiveness of this bet pattern. We now have half of the point numbers covered, all at risk of being repeated and thereby lost. However, if we've successfully established all 3 don't numbers with full double odds laid against and the 7 is rolled, we collect on all bets. Let's follow one short roll of the dice to illustrate this pattern. The disc is "off" and we're coming out. We bet $10 on the don't pass line, and the dice are thrown:

Come out Roll	7	Lose $10 don't pass bet. Replace with $10.
Come out Roll	3 (craps)	Win $10 don't pass bet. Remove $10 winnings to rails.
Come out Roll	5 (point)	Lay $30 against the point. Make a $10 don't come bet.
1st Come Roll	2 (craps)	Win $10 on the don't come bet.
2nd Come Roll	10	The dealer moves our don't come bet to the 10. We lay $40

		against the 10. Make another $10 don't come bet.
Next Come Roll	8	Lay $24 against the 8.

At this point we have three don't numbers established, the 5 as our point and the 10 and 8 as our don't come numbers, representing a total of $124 on the layout. With three numbers established we stop betting. Let's continue:

Next Come Roll	8	Lose $34 on the don't come bet on the 8. ($10 plus $24 in double odds.) Bet $10 in the don't come Box.
Next Come Roll	6	Lay $24 in double odds against 6.
Next Come Roll	4	No effect on our bets.
Next Come Roll	11	No effect on our bets.
Next Come Roll	7	Win $30 on point of 5. ($10 plus $20 in odds at 2-3.) Win $30 on don't come no. of 10. ($10 plus $20 at 1-2.) Win $30 on don't come no. of 6. ($10 plus $20 at 5-6.)

Let's summarize the action. We lost $10 on the first 7 and $34 on the don't come number 8 that repeated. We won $20 on two craps and $90 on the final roll of 7. Total rolls in the game were 11.

Result:	
Total Wins	$110
Total Loses	44
Net Win	$ 66

You'll notice over time that wins on the "don't" side tend to be a little slower and more steady than wins on the "do" side which tend to be more explosive. Again, your personality and comfort level should guide you in deciding which side you favor.

Don't Pass Bet with Two Don't Come Bets
All with Full Double Odds
Assisted with Field Bets and Lay
Wagers on the 4 and 10
(Wrong Side—Most Aggressive)

Now is a good time to go back and review field bets and lay wagers, particularly how to improve the odds on lay wagers.

Let's again review our 3% rule: never make a bet that gives the house more than 3% advantage. The closer the house advantage is to 3%, the less frequently we employ it. If the field paid double on both the 2 and 12 we would never use it, as the house advantage jumps to 5.55%. I rarely suggest this daring bet pattern but if we have a field that pays triple on either the 2 or 12 and we feel a table is cold, this bet could prove fruitful. For if the table proves cold, this pattern will be the most effective way to profit while holding the line on the house edge.

Here we begin in a similar fashion to the previous bet pattern, making one don't pass bet followed by 2 don't come bets and laying double odds on all. However, on a come out roll we make a field bet of the same size as our don't pass bet. Once the point is established we pull down our field bet. This is a built-in way to limit the frequency of using the field bet— only make it on come out rolls. If the shooter has a typical run of between 5 and 12 rolls, then we would be employing the field bet about 10% to 20% of the time. This is manageable. If the table is cold and we're coming out with frequent craps and outside numbers, this start will add nicely to our profits.

Let's examine this part of our bet pattern for a moment. Assume we have $10 on the line (don't pass) with a matching $10 on the field. Consider the following:

Coming out with $10 Don't Pass Bet and $10 Field bet

Number Thrown	Result	Reaction
2 (Craps)	$10 win don't pass bet. $20 double win in the Field.	Remove winnings, leave both bets up.
3 (Craps)	$10 win don't pass bet. $10 win in the field.	Remove winnings, leave both bets up.
4 (Point)	$10 on point of 4. $10 win in the field.	Lay double odds against the 4. Remove field bet with winnings.
5 (Point)	$10 on point of 5. $10 loss in the field.	Lay double odds against 5.
6 (point)	$10 on point of 6. $10 loss in the field.	Lay double odds against the 6.
7 (Natural)	$10 loss on don't pass. $10 loss in the field.	Replace both bets.
8 (Point)	$10 on point of 8. $10 loss in the field.	Lay double odds against the 8.
9 (Point)	$10 on point of 9. $10 win in the field.	Lay double odds against the 9. Remove field bet with winnings.
10 (Point)	$10 on point of 10. $10 win in the field.	Lay double odds against the 10. Remove field bet with winnings.
11 (Natural)	$10 loss on don't pass. $10 win in Field.	Shift field bet win back to the don't pass line.
12 (Craps)	$10 Push on don't pass. $30 win in Field.	Remove field bet winnings, leave both bets up.

As you can see, when outside numbers are thrown this gives us a strong start. For example, if we come out with a 10, we win our field bet, pick it up along with the winnings, and we have a nice "No Ten" as our point. Only when the 7 is thrown on the come out roll would we lose both bets. Study the chart and practice this at home and see if you're comfortable with the dynamics of this beginning. Keep in mind that the house edge must be restrained to reasonable levels.

After we've established our don't pass point number we make our two don't come bets and lay full double odds against all numbers. Again, we remind you that with any "don't" bet pattern you must protect against any substantial loss due to a hot roll. Always follow this rule: if the point repeats (a losing bet for the don't bettor) only replace it one time. Similarly, if the don't come numbers repeat, only replace each once. If a don't come number repeats a second time just stand back and wait for the shooter to 7 out. Laying double odds is by far the best way to play the don't side. But stubbornly continuing to replace lost bets will be the ruin of any "don't" bettor because hot rolls do occur. Let them run their course. Remember the adage: "He who fights and runs away lives to fight another day." don't ever break this rule.

Having said that, this bet pattern gives us a certain flexibility. If during play we lose a don't come toss, we can replace it by placing a lay wager against either the 4 or 10 instead of following up with a don't come bet. Remember, we want to continue with three numbers up. The $10 bettor, laying double odds against the 4 or 10 as a don't come bet, would make a lay wager by giving the dealer $50 as a "No 4" or "No 10" lay wager. The commission would be $1. If the 7 comes now, we would get back our $50, plus $25 in winnings on the lay wagers. If the 10 (or 4) were to repeat, thereby losing our lay wager, we would stop betting and wait for the shooter to 7 out.

Let's go through a short roll series to illustrate this aggressive wrong side betting pattern. The disc is "off" and we're coming out. We bet $10 on the don't pass line and $10 in the field.

Come out Roll	2 (craps)	$10 win on don't pass. $20 win in field. Pick up winnings. Leave both bets.
2nd Come out Roll	9	$10 win in field. Lay $30 in double odds against the 9. Pick up field bet and winnings.
1st Come Roll	11	$10 loss on the don't come bet. Replace it.
2nd Come Roll	3 (craps)	$10 win on don't come bet. Remove winnings, leave bet up.

| 3rd Come Roll | 4 | Lay $40 in double odds against 4. Make a $10 don't come bet. |
| Next Come Roll | 6 | Lay $24 against the 6, stop betting. |

At this point we have net winnings of $40 with a point of 9 and two don't come numbers of 4 and 6 all with double odds against, so we stop betting. Let's continue:

Next Come Roll	12 (craps)	No effect on our bets.
Next Come Roll	11	No effect on our bets.
Next Come Roll	8	No effect on our bets.
Next Come Roll	6	$34 loss on don't come number 6. Make a lay wager of $50 against the 10 ($1 commission.)
Next Come Roll	5	No effect on our bets.
Next Come Roll	7	$30 win on point of 9, $30 win on don't come point of 4. $25 win on lay wager 10 less $1 commission paid.

The results of our betting are that we lost $10 on an 11 and $34 on the don't come number 6 that repeated and we paid $1 in commission on the "no ten" lay wager. We won $30 in the field, $20 in craps thrown, $30 on the point, $30 on the don't come bet on the 4 and $25 on the "no ten" lay wager with a total of 12 rolls.

Result:

Total Wins	$135
Total Loses	45
Net Win	$ 90

I was playing in Lake Tahoe a few years ago when a I saw a man play similarly to the above pattern, with $50 bets. He walked up to the table, bought one thousand dollars worth of chips, and very calmly put $50 in the field and $50 on the don't pass line. He would then lay double odds against the point and pick up his field bet. He would then make one more don't come bet and lay double odds against it. The dice were moderately cold and I watched him make about $500 in fifteen minutes. Before he left I commented to him "that's an interesting way to play". He responded "It's simple. I just bet with the house". There is a common misconception that one is betting "with the house" when betting the don't side. In this particular instance he was also including the field bet as betting "with the house". Now, as we know, he is technically incorrect. You can't bet with the house. The house books all bets and maintains an advantage on all of them. On the don't side the house will win the pass line bets when the 12 is thrown where the don't side bettor is barred from winning. Therein lies the house's edge. But nonetheless, he stuck with a very specific pattern that effectively limited the house's percentage. And, with good money management, he could be very successful.

Whatever bet pattern you feel comfortable with, we strongly recommend you first practice at home. See "Practice Makes Perfect" in chapter 9.

Chapter Summary

Good craps players take the little time necessary to learn both sides of the dice in order to take advantage of trends as they occur. When constructing bet patterns players should always stay within the constraints of the 3% rule. Bet patterns can range from conservative to aggressive, all the while keeping the house edge restrained to reasonable levels. Ultimately, the bet patterns that you construct for yourself are a reflection of your personality, knowledge of the game, and risk tolerance. Always practice a particular pattern at home until you feel comfortable with it before attempting live play at the casino.

CHAPTER SEVEN

Bet Progression

By intelligently constructing your bet patterns you can effectively hold the casino's advantage down to manageable levels. You can virtually meet the casino head-on, statistically speaking. However, the key to winning explosively while keeping risk exposure to reasonable minimums is bet progression.

Any credible writer, gambler, or theorist will agree on this one vital rule: Never increase your bet size when losing—only when winning. Refer back to Chapter 5 on understanding streaks, for it is through intelligent management of both winning and losing streaks that consistent and long term winning is possible.

Chapter 5 demonstrates the damage that can be done if you raise your bets upon losses. But let's turn this around. If serious damage can occur by increasing bet size when losing, doesn't it following that explosive wins can occur if we were to systematically increase our bets upon wins? As we'll see, clearly this is the case. One quick caveat: the beginner player should stick with level betting sizes whether winning or losing before employing bet progression until he is very comfortable with live play. Practice progressions at home before attempting them in live play.

Consider the following chart that depicts the effects on ones bankroll should a losing streak occur versus what will happen should a winning streak occur maintaining a level bet size. Assume a $10 bet, taking double odds with points of only the 6 or 8. The bankroll (bankrolling will be discussed fully in the next chapter) to cover one number would be about $210. We will bet $10 and maintain a level bet size upon winning. We will denote this progression as 10pt–10pt–10pt. This means that every time the point repeats (wins) we maintain the same bet size on the following bet.

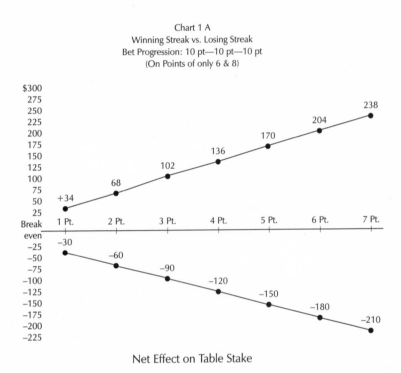

Chart 1 A
Winning Streak vs. Losing Streak
Bet Progression: 10 pt—10 pt—10 pt
(On Points of only 6 & 8)

Net Effect on Table Stake

Let's examine the loss line first.

If we bet $10 on the pass line and the point were 6, we would take double odds of $20 for a total bet of $30. If the 7 comes before the point—a loss for us—we'd be down $30 and make the same bet again. If we lost again we'd be down a total of $60 and so on. If we were to lose 7 points in a row (a very rare occurrence) we would have lost $210 or our entire bankroll.

Now let's examine the win line. A $10 bet backed with double odds on the 6 would again be $30. If we won, we would win $34 and make a new pass line bet of $10, again taking double odds. If we won 2 points we'd be ahead $68, and so on. After 7 points made we'd be ahead $238. Bear in mind that we're playing only the 6 and 8. If we were using points of 5 and 9, or 4 and 10, our win line would ascend substantially faster while our loss line would stay the same. For example, if the 5 were our first point we would have still bet only $10 with $20 in odds for a total of $30 at risk. If the 5 repeated our win would be $10 on the basic bet plus $30 on the odds bet of $20 at 3-2 for a total win of $40! If the point were 4 or 10 the total win would be $50.

Now let's observe the effect of bet progression following wins. We'll use the following bet progressions of 10pt–20pt–30pt (illustrated in chart 1B). This means we will increase our bets by $10 on each win. Again, we'll use only points of 6 and 8, covering only one number, and of course we always keep our bets at the minimum level when losing.

There are two factors you should note. First of all, and very importantly, the loss line remains the same as in the last chart where we did not increase bets upon winning. Again, we always maintain our minimum bet after losses—in this case $10 plus $20 in odds. Secondly, we see our win line moves up at an exponential rate. Again, bear in mind this is only on points of 6 or 8. On the outside numbers this ascent would be substantially more dramatic. Now, to be completely pragmatic about this we must take into account the fact that even on a winning streak we will eventually lose the last bet which will necessarily be at an increased level. On the following chart (1C) we've added the line depicting the net effect on our bankroll when we eventually lose our final progressed bet which will most likely end our session.

As you'll see now, our win line, when we consider the final progressed bet lost, runs below the win line when we don't consider that final lost bet. Further, if we win our first point and lose the second point, we will actually experience a net loss of $26.

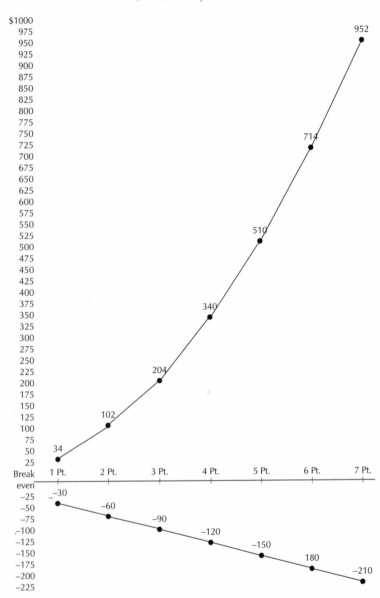

Chart 1B
Winning Streak vs. Losing Streak
Bet Progression: 10 pt—20 pt—30 pt
(On Points of only 6 & 8)

Net Effect on Table Stake

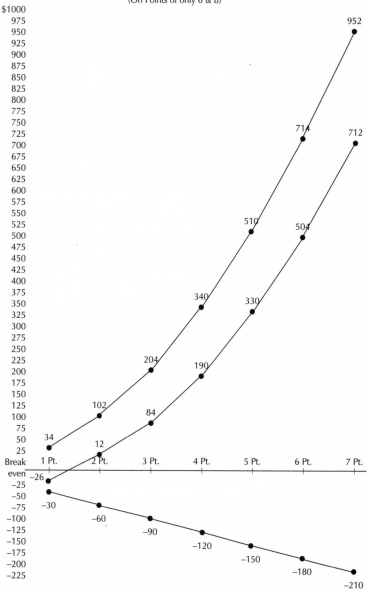

Chart 1C
Winning Streak vs. Losing Streak
Bet Progression: 10 pt—20 pt—30 pt
With Effect of final Losing bet
(On Points of only 6 & 8)

Net Effect on Table Stake

Not until 3 points are made do we do better than our level betting counterpart. After three points are won we see that bet progression far out performs level betting.

It bears repeating again that these charts deal only with the 6 and 8 as points and that when outside numbers are repeated the resulting profits will be profoundly higher. And when running this bet progression on a pass line bet and then on the come as previously suggested, the profits on a hot roll can be explosive. In this situation we would treat each bet individually. If one number repeated it would be followed with the increased bet whether it was a pass line or come bet. Therefore, in the middle of a hot roll wagers may be at different levels.

Modifications to Straight Bet Progression

When playing 3 numbers, 1 pass line and 2 come numbers, there are choices available to improve on simple straight bet progression.

Increase Bets at a Decreasing Rate

If the dice begin to "chop" (alternate between winning and losing) we will experience a decline in our bankroll. On progressions of $10pt–$20pt–$30pt, etc., we'll lose $26 after every two bets where the points were 6 or 8 even though we were winning 50% of the time. In this progression we increase our bets by $10 upon wins. After our first win we increase our wager one hundred percent to $20. This is a substantial jump. If the bet is won, we move from $20 up to $30; a 50% increase. If the $30 bet is won, our next bet would be $40 or a 33% increase, and so on. So, we see that by increasing the bet by a fixed amount, in this case $10, we are increasing at a decreasing rate. However, the problem here is with our first increase from $10 to $20, a one hundred percent increase. When the line bet is combined with double odds this is quite aggressive. Our $10 bet with double odds of $20 totals $30. By increasing our second bet less than one hundred percent we move a little more conservatively. Maintaining a similar bet size one might progress as follows; 10pt–15pt–20pt–25pt etc. This progression would still yield a nice win during a hot roll and would lessen the negative effects of chopping dice.

One might consider 20pt–30pt–40pt, etc. Here we're starting with a bigger bet but we begin increasing at a decreasing rate. The larger bettor might try 50pt–75pt–100pt or, perhaps 500pt–750pt–1,000pt. Whatever your bet, experience has shown the best progression is to increase at a decreasing rate in order to stem the effect of chopping while having an upside potential should a hot roll develop. Again, as with bet amount and bet pattern, progression is a matter of personal comfort level. Choose wisely.

Increase Bets Only When the Point is Made

Some very good players suggest treating every bet—whether a pass line or a come—as an individual bet. If any bet is won, the follow up bet is increased. If the follow-up bet also wins, then its follow-up bet is increased to the third level. Meanwhile, the other bets remain at the lower level, and are only increased if and when they win.

It could be argued that to progress bets this way is too aggressive and requires a very long hot roll to show a profit, at which time, of course, the profits would indeed soar. Remember, the faster you increase, the more aggressive the strategy.

If playing a pass line bet with 2 come numbers, consider increasing your wager only after the point is made. Then we follow it up with an increased bet on the next come out roll. In the progression 10 pt–15 pt–20 pt–25 pt, our second line bet would be $15. Now, with the pass line bet at $15, our come bets remain at $10 each. But now as the come bets repeat they will be increased to match the pass line bet of $15 (of course all wagers are backed by double odds). If the come bets are repeated again before the pass line wins again they are followed up with $15 come bets again matching the pass line bet.

Should the pass line (the point) repeat a second time, the next is increased to $20. And now, as our $15 come bets are repeated and won, they are replaced with $20 bets (matching the pass line) and so on.

This is a very deliberate and intelligent way to progress one's bets. And remember the advantage on all come out rolls with an increased line bet. With our place bets and odds on come bets off on the come out roll, the 7 now becomes far less of a threat. For example, let's follow the following progression for our $10 bettor. The disc is "off" and we're coming out. We bet $10 on the pass line.

Come Out Roll	9 (point)	Back up with $20 odds, make a $10 come bet.
1st Come Roll	6	Back up with $20 odds, make a $10 come bet.
2nd Come Roll	5	Back up with $20 odds. Stop betting.
Next Come Roll	2 (craps)	No effect on our bets.
Next Come Roll	5	Win $40, make a $10 come bet.
Next Come Roll	4	Back up with $20 odds. Stop betting.
Next Come Roll	9 (point)	Win $40.

Let's pause for a moment. Our original pattern called for 3 numbers to be covered with double odds on each for approximately $90 at risk. So far, we've won $80 and now we follow up with our increased pass line bet of $15. If we see the 7 now on this come out roll we'll lose both come bets of $10 each; the odds on the come bets are returned to us; and we will win the larger $15 pass line bet for a net loss on the roll of only $5 and the layout is cleared. The game netted us a $75 win in 8 rolls. Further, if we were playing a little more aggressively with place bets up, they would have been off as well.

With the dice passing, we would want to continue play. Whether to continue at a $10 or $15 level is strictly a matter of choice. But you should see the advantage of "sevening out" on a come roll with an increased pass line bet. Over time, this difference will be substantial versus making the same size pass line bet or increasing your come bets individually and then sevening out.

Level Off Bet Progression

If you will recall Chapter 5 on understanding streaks you'll remember the potential for disaster when you double up upon losing—as is done in the famous and bogus Martingale system of betting. The $10 bettor who bets $20 then $40 then $80 and so on, will have lost $1,270 after 7 consecutive losses. If we reverse this thinking and take an anti-Martingale approach, it would stand to reason that we could make explosive profit if we were to leave our winnings up or "let it ride" on wins. The $10 bettor would win $10 and bet a total of $20 on the second bet. If he won again he would then have a total of $40 and then bet that and so on. If he won 7 times in a row his $10 bet would have multiplied to $1,280 or a $1,270 profit! If he continued "letting it ride" it is clear that ultimately, when he did lose, he would lose all including his initial $10 bet. Obviously, to be practical, he would have to, at some point during the winning streak, either stop betting and walk away with profits or at least level off the wager size. In this way he would be assured of winning if he hit a pre-determined number of wins.

If we apply this thinking to our wagering progressions, you will see the advantage of leveling off bets at some point, but still continuing to bet until a loss occurs. If we level off our bets, which is to say that we are constantly setting aside some of our gains, we end the session without substantial damage to our profits when a winning streak ends.

The aggressive player may do very well by simply establishing a progression that increases at a decreasing rate as determined in the previous section. To be a bit more conservative you may choose to level off the bet size after 2 or 3 points are made. One might decide to employ the following bet progression: 20pt–30pt–40pt–40pt . This denotes starting with a $20 bet on the pass line and then, when the first point is made, we go to $30. If the second point is made we go to $40 and continue with $40 bets until the shooter sevens out. This is a bit more conservative than a straight, unlimited progression but will yield a nicer win on just a moderately warm roll while still leaving the total upside unlimited.

Bet Progression on the Don't Side

As with any progression we always keep our bets at a minimum to control damage during losing streaks which do inevitably occur. But how do we progress our bets when winning on the don't side? First we must choose our bet pattern. For example, we'll bet one don't pass bet followed by 2 don't come numbers. Here, what the wrong side bettor endeavors to do is to establish all 3 numbers, one don't pass and 2 don't come, and lay double odds against all three hoping the shooter sevens out before any of the numbers repeat thereby winning all three bets. Now we have to reverse our thinking here from right side betting. If all 3 bets are won we would increase our bet on the next come out roll to some predetermined maximum amount. However, if we were to lose one number and then win only 2 or even all 3 (after reestablishing the last point) we'd settle for a lower increase. Here again, we strongly suggest increasing at a decreasing rate. Let's use an example. If we start at $20, we establish the 3 numbers and lay double odds on all. If we win all 3 bets—by the shooter sevening out—the table would be cleared and we'd move up to a $30 wager. If we were to establish 3 numbers again and win all 3, we would go to $40 and then stay at $40 until a hot roll cleared our bets. Now, on the other hand, if we lost one number in the first game, before the shooter 7'd out we would only increase to $25 instead of $30 for the next game. If two numbers were lost before the Shooter 7'd out, we would not increase our bets. Remember, we want to keep our bets at a minimum while the dice are against us.

Consider the following chart that the $20 bettor would follow with a basic bet progression of 20pt–30pt–40pt, playing one don't pass bet with two don't come bets.

Win all 3 bets	= Begin next roll at $30
Lose 1 number	= Then win all 3 = increase wager to only $25
Lose 2 numbers	= Begin next game at $20 (original wager)
Lose 3 numbers	= Begin next game at $20
Lose 4 or 5 numbers	= Consider switching to pass line or simply leave that table.

Keep in mind your protection against the hot roll: only replace 1 don't come bet if one is lost and only replace 1 don't pass bet if it is lost. This guarantees a maximum loss of only 5 numbers—worst case scenario—on any one hot roll.

Let's look at an example. The disc is off and we bet $20 on the don't pass line.

Come out Roll	9 (point)	Lay $60 in double odds behind the don't pass bet. Bet $20 in the don't come box.
1st Come Roll	8	Lay $48 in double odds on the 8. Bet $20 in the don't come box
2nd Come Roll	4	Lay $80 in double odds against the 4. Stop betting.

Now, with 3 numbers established, if the 7 were thrown we would win all our bets and the table would be cleared. We would bet against the next shooter at the maximum next level bet of $30. We would then strive to establish 3 new numbers with full double odds on all bets at this level. If we 7'd out again, we would move to $40 and stay there until we had a losing roll. Let's continue on the premise that we lose a number.

Next Come Roll	8	Lose $68 on the 8. Bet $20 in the don't come box.
Next Roll	5	Lay $60 against 5.
Next Roll	7	Win.

Now we've won 3 numbers, but after losing one number we increase our bet only $5 to $25. We continue with the same bet progression; if we established 3 numbers all with double odds and won all three we would move up $10 to $35 and stay at this level until the shooter had a hot roll. As long as the dice stay cold, we'll keep at this level on the don't side until the cows come home.

If you're interested in don't betting, re-read this section and practice this progression with your comfortable wager at home. As always, rolls of craps and eleven have no effect on our progression. With this pattern and progression you're keeping the house edge pared to the bare minimum of .6% while keeping bets at a minimum when losing and increasing them while winning. That's good gambling and smart play.

Chapter Summary

Intelligent bet progressions are the key to explosive wins at craps. The faster one increases one's bets upon wins, the more aggressive the strategy. The rate at which a player increases his bets is a function of his own personality and posture at the table. Players should always maintain their minimum wagers during losing streaks.

CHAPTER EIGHT

Bankroll and Money Managements

Thus far we have discussed in detail three crucial components of winning at craps: statistically correct betting, constructing effective patterns, and incorporating intelligent progressions that can lead to explosive wins while minimizing losses. But there is another vital component that is often disregarded though it is integral to professional play and long term success.

Bankroll and money management, a relatively simple concept, is overlooked by the vast majority of gamblers—whatever their game might be. I've seen players walk up to a table with $100 and make $25 bets. Unless the dice do exactly what such a player wants, he'll be gone in 4 or 5 rolls. If anyone thinks he can predict the next 5 rolls of the dice, he should immediately seek help at the nearest gamblers anonymous chapter. The player betting this way is not even giving himself a chance at winning. He is literally playing simply to see how long he can go before he loses. I've seen players walk to the table and pull out a thousand dollars, lose it within twenty minutes, and then throw another thousand on the table and twenty minutes later yet another. Is this player playing professionally? What are his policies? What defines a losing session for him? What defines a win? These are important questions that anyone striving to play professionally should resolve long before approaching the table. We're not encouraging anyone to gamble. But gambling is a legitimate form of entertainment if done intelligently.

First of all, no one should ever play with money they can't afford to lose. You should not play with money needed for essentials such as rent or food or family expenses. This behavior tempts disaster and disaster surely will result. Gambling is a matter of risk versus reward. If one takes his last $800 to the tables in hopes of doubling his money then he should weigh the $800 upside potential against the downside potential which may be eviction from his apartment! This clearly is not a balanced risk-versus-reward proposition, no matter how skillful the play.

Once you have objectively determined the amount of money you can risk with virtually no impact on your current or future life circumstances, then you are ready to attack the casinos head on.

Bankrolling

Bankrolling can be broken into two parts: the bankroll you take to the table to adequately fund your bet size (the table stake), and the total bankroll required to fund your outing. Simply stated, for pass line players the table stake should be between five and seven times one full cycle of betting, while the total bankroll should be sufficient to allow play over a certain period of time (an outing).

Let's first consider the table stake. We'll start with an example using "units" bet, and then illustrate this with an example using dollars. If a player bets 2 units on the pass line, he would be making an odds bet of 4 units behind the line for a total of 6 units bet. If his pattern were to follow the pass line bet with 2 come bets, both backed with double odds, then one cycle of betting would be 18 units. This would mean the player should bring a table stake of between five and seven times 18 units or between 90 and 126 units.

Now lets use cold cash so you can see how this system really works. If the player is using $5 chips and making 2 unit bets of $10 with $20 odds, then 1 pass line bet with 2 come bets would total $90 for one full cycle. His table stake should be between five and seven times this amount or $450 to $630. The $10 bettor (2 unit bets with $5 chips) can easily play for a long time, even when the dice go against him, if he begins with this kind of appropriate amount. This allows ample time for a hot roll to develop at which time, with an intelligent bet progression, the player will win nicely and maybe big. The player who is under-capitalized generally won't stay at the table long enough for a hot roll to develop, especially if he's making bad bets (those wagers that give the house greater than a 3% advantage). If one were betting $100 on three numbers, all with double odds, then one cycle would be $900. In this case the player's table stake should be between $4,500 and $6,300. If a $10 bettor were playing only two numbers, then one cycle would be $60. His table stake should be somewhere between $300 and $420.

There are similar rules for don't bettors: the table stake should equal five to seven times one cycle of betting. This takes a little more thought because the amount of one cycle depends on which point and don't come numbers are established. For example, if we're betting 2 units on the don't pass line, then points of no 4 and no 10 would require 8 units laid as odds; the no 5 and no 9 would require 6 units; the no 6 and no 8 would require about 5 units. You might just base the table stake around a point and 2 come numbers of no 4, no 5, and no 6. One cycle would require about 25 units. Five to seven times 25 units would be 125 to 175 units. Our $10 bettor would need between $625 and $875 as his table stake to be properly capitalized. If you walk to a table capitalized in this manner with the recommended bet patterns and appropriate wagers, the boxman, crew and floorman will see that you're a serious player who knows the game.

The bankroll for an outing is based around the table stake. Whether you're going out for a brief evening on one of the riverboats (which are so numerous today) or for a long weekend in Vegas, Tahoe or Atlantic City, you will determine your bankroll from the table stake. The total bankroll for the outing should equal the table stake times the number of gaming sessions anticipated per day times the number of days of gambling. Let's say you visit Las Vegas for three days of gambling. If you anticipate two gaming sessions per day, then you would want to bring an amount equal to your table stake times six. The $10 bettor who determines his table stake to be $600 should bring $3,600 with him. If you anticipated two sessions the first day and three each of the next two days, you would bring $600 X 8, or $4,800. To some, this will sound like more money than they would ever have expected the game to require. Certainly, to the recreational player, proper bankrolling is not really a major factor. But proper bankrolling is an integral ingredient for the professional or serious player who is committed to winning over the long pull. He knows that it can take time to work a table, waiting for that hot roll to develop. He knows that one must lay in wait and then pounce on the hot streak by systematically progressing bets for an explosive win. The pro knows that the normal volatility of the game will sometimes dig into the table stake and the total bankroll and that he will have to absorb losses while waiting to capitalize on gains. You can't go to Las Vegas for 3 days with $500 and expect to engage in any real action, let alone have a reasonable chance to win.

At some point the seasoned and disciplined player might determine an outing's bankroll this way: The number of sessions anticipated the first day times the table stake plus the number of sessions the second day times the table stake times one half, plus the number of sessions the third day times the table stake times one quarter. In our example above of two sessions per day, we would take $1,200 for the first day plus $600 for the second day plus $300 for the third day for a total bankroll of $2,100. However, when just starting serious play we strongly recommend staying closer to the higher end of the limits laid out above.

Recreational or amateur players can do anything they want while hoping and praying to shatter the odds—the gaming cities and riverboats thrive on this kind of shot-in-the-dark play. Professional players, however, are properly capitalized and monitor their play and bankrolls just as efficiently as the casinos themselves do.

Money Management

Once you have established your table stake and bankroll for the outing, you must learn to manage this money properly and with constancy if you want the best chance of seeing this money grow.

The first rule of successful gambling is never to take a devastating loss. Never get swept up in the emotion of the game when on a losing streak. Don't pray for luck to quickly recap losses while pulling out more and more money. The one sure way to be certain you'll never take a beating is to never lose more than your table stake at any one gaming session. If your table stake is gone—its time to quit. Pull the plug on the session. Go for a walk, take in a show or get a bite to eat, but don't ever reach into your pocket and pull out more money on a losing streak. Let's go one step further. If you ever find that you don't have enough money to cover one full cycle of bets, just walk away. If one cycle of bets equals $90 and you have only $80 left in the rails—pick up and cash out. Over time that $80 saved adds up. If you had 8 losing sessions where you left with $80 instead of nothing, that would total $640 saved—enough for one fully capitalized session. It would be virtually impossible to fight your way back to a win with a table stake so crippled that you can't execute your bet pattern. Throw in the towel. The casinos work a twenty-four hour day. You can't win every time, no matter how sharp you are. Don't ever get killed! Limiting losses is as key to long term winning as winning itself is. Don't get sucked into the bottomless pit of a losing streak where you just can't get on the right side of the dice. Healthy wins can be wiped out by one gigantic uncontrolled loss. If your personality is one that demands a win every time you play and you are unable to stop until you do win—then put this book down and vow to never gamble again. A successful gaming session is not merely measured by whether or not you've won. A successful session is measured by how well you stick to your policies—win or lose. Learn to accept small losses. One can almost come to enjoy them as part of the game. If there was no risk of loss it wouldn't be gambling!

If you cash in at a table and you're a right bettor with 3 numbers and you get 3 numbers up and 7 out, then 3 numbers up and 7 out again, and then maybe a third time, you might consider stopping right there. We call this "short stopping". In this case you would have only lost less than half your table stake. Maybe that's enough. Don't fight the tide. Learn to take small losses, it will prove to be one of your most valuable tactics. And don't forget—as easy as it is to get caught on a losing streak, it's equally easy to get caught on a winning streak, at which time you'll systematically progress your bet and net a comfortable profit.

Maximizing Wins

From time to time the dice do exactly what you would have them do. The chips start piling up in the rails as number after number repeats. And now comes the critical question: when do you stop? The policies that you develop that determine when you end a winning session will, in large part, determine your success. The psychological mechanisms involved in gaming are powerful. When one is winning, the emotional high can be so overwhelming that it can prove impossible to leave the table. You believe you've mastered the game and your good luck won't change. The psychology can be just as overwhelming when losing. The player can believe luck must turn around eventually and he can become desperate to recoup growing losses with every throw of the dice. This can continue until the player is just flat out of money, thereby ending the session in the unhappiest of ways.

How many times I've heard players lament "I was up (x amount of dollars) at one point—if only I would have stopped then!" They go on to say they ended up flat broke. It seems that most players, especially recreational or amateur players, are unwilling to win, stopping play only when at the bottom of their undefined bankroll. The bottom is easily reached when consistently poor, statistically weak bets are made. So what's the rule for ending winning sessions with a win? The right bettor should consistently quit the table at the end of a hot roll. The Right bettor plays in anticipation of a hot roll and can watch his table stake rise and fall for an hour or two while doing so. When it does come the player should ride it out all the way and then depart instantly when it ends. Cash out and be willing to leave with profits. This sounds easier to do than it actually is, but is a must for long-term winning.

So what constitutes a hot roll? There are a couple of ways to determine this. You might consider it a hot roll when a player has held the dice for, say, thirty minutes or more. To do this keep an eye on your watch with the starting roll of each new shooter. Then when a thirty minutes roll is acheived, you continue play until the shooter 7's out. You could determine a hot roll or winning session based on some function of your table stake. For example, if you make 50% or 100% of your table stake then you would continue play and leave when the hot shooter 7's out. Here you'll need to keep close watch on your chips to know exactly when you've hit your win goal. But again, the right bettor should never leave during a hot roll— always wait until the shooter 7's out! You never know how long a roll can go and you want to get the maximum benefits of the roll and then quit when the seven shows.

The preferred way to interpret a hot roll when playing the pass line works like this: when the shooter has made two con- secutive points, it's a hot roll. Now, you might not believe that making two points constitutes a hot roll, but I'm not advising you to stop at this time. Remember that you never leave until the hot roll is over. The shooter may go on to hit five or ten points or more, all the while hitting a succession of winning come numbers and placed sixes and eights, netting a sizeable win. Admittedly, if the shooter makes two points and then immediately 7's out, this will probably not be a great win, unless a bunch of come numbers hit in the mean time. But it's still a win. Any small win is better than any loss. Playing this way will increase the frequency of quitting a winner while continuing the opportunity to exploit a hot roll. The point here is that the professional player has clearly defined a win for himself before beginning play and is ready to walk away from the table with that win intact—big or small! Remember this: pigs get fat but hogs get slaughtered. When you've experienced a sufficient win, don't become greedy and try to break the casino or you might find yourself penned up with the hogs.

For the don't bettor, the best way to define a win is based on the bankroll. The player might define a win as gaining fifty percent of his original table stake. At this point he should go on some sort of G & E (see next section on Guarantee & Excess). Once you've made your win goal, stop and walk away a winner. But remember, only walk away after the current streak has run its course.

Guarantee & Excess

Guarantee & Excess is a theory in gaming where the player can "guarantee" a win by committing to playing with only a part of profit currently in hand and stopping when that allotment is lost. Here, once the win goal is acheived the original table stake should be set aside. You then take your profit and subtract chips necessary to cover one cycle of bets, establishing your "guaranteed" win. The chips you put in play for one cycle's worth of bets would be your "excess". Any further winnings would be moved over to the "guarantee" and you play with one cycle's worth. If you continue winning, then those chips would become part of the guarantee and play would again continue with the excess. For example, the "don't" bettor might establish a win goal to be fifty percent of his original table stake. Once fifty percent of his bankroll is made the player would set his original stake plus the winnings to one side of the rails and isolate enough chips for one cycle of bets. If the table stays cold (he keeps winning) then he would continue to take profits and add them to the "guarantee" while continuing to play with one cycle's worth. If he were to run into an endless succession of point, 7, point, 7, he would keep playing. Anything gained over one cycle's worth is added to the "guarantee". He'd continue this until the don't bets got picked off, at which time he would pickup and cash out. Again, once he has hit his win goal and established his guarantee he should never touch those chips but only ride out the streak by playing exclusively with the "excess" established to play one cycle of bets.

Guarantee & Excess is an important theory that, once mastered, will enhance a player's overall performance.

Chapter Summary

Bankroll and money management is the fourth and final element that must be incorporated into successful play. Bankrolling can be broken down into two parts: the table stake and the total bankroll available for gaming. The table stake is determined from the bet size and bet pattern involved in making one cycle of bets. The total bankroll available for gaming is a function of the table stake and the number of sessions that are anticipated.

Money management deals with maximizing wins by defining a win and limiting losses by suspending play when faced with losing streaks.

CHAPTER NINE

Winning Consistently:
The Professional Player

At this point, the differences between the recreational or amateur gambler (which includes approximately 99% of all players) and the professional player should be clear. Recreational players characteristically:

- play for thrills, usually with high hopes for a win, but expect to lose;
- have read a book or two on the game, at best, but have never really followed through by practicing or developing winning strategies;
- have never defined a win or a loss and easily get swept up emotionally in the game, quickly abandoning any intelligent planning they might have done;
- play inconsistently (e.g. twice in a week then not for six months) and when they do, play hunches and intuitions with no real direction or discernable betting plan;
- make bets that have large potential payoffs but offer excess percentage advantages to the house;
- are substantially under-capitalized and play erratic bet patterns, frequently increasing bets when losing;
- are riddled with superstition and feel they can cause good luck or avoid bad luck based on their actions or what they wear or by some other means;
- take advantage of the free alcoholic drinks.

The professional player, on the other hand:

- has decided to play for consistent profits;
- has taken the time necessary to study the game and to become familiar with the statistics and percentages, at least on the low house percentage bets;
- has objectively calculated discretionary funds and has properly figured his bankroll, table stake, and bet sizes;
- has defined wins and losses along with constructing statistically correct patterns, long before he approaches a table and engages in live play;
- has developed proper money management skills in order to regularly maximize gains and minimize losses;
- plays consistently and only when he feels ready both physically and emotionally
- has left superstition to the amateurs and has realized that neither good luck nor bad luck can be caused or avoided by deliberate actions
- never drinks alcohol while playing

Luck vs. Superstition

It is important that the professional player distinguishes between luck and superstition and understands how each one effects games of chance.

First of all, luck does exist. Luck occurs when the outcome of a particular event or particular procession of events does not manifest the way the odds would indicate, and the result is to the benefit of the player. For example, lets go back to our coin flipping friend of chapter 3. Our friend was giving us $9 each time the coin came up tails and we were giving him $10 each time the coin came up heads on a total of ten flips. The odds would indicate the coin would most likely come up heads five times and tails five times. If the actual outcome were four heads and six tails it could be said that we got lucky as we beat the odds and ultimately won $14. Had the actual outcome been five heads and five tails, as the odds indicate should happen, we would lose $5. Now, in this case we would not say we were unlucky because we lost $5. It would be more accurate to say that we lost $5 because we made a bad bet!

Superstition, on the other hand, is the belief that one can cause good luck or avoid bad luck based on some external stimuli. This can cause players to take the most ridiculous steps, such as wearing a certain shirt or baseball cap when playing or ritualistically rubbing the dice a certain way each and every time they throw them.

This kind of behavior not only interferes with good gaming but can also be needlessly annoying to others around the table. Dice have no memory and no vested interest in the outcome of the game and are certainly unaffected by any external stimuli. They are just two mindless plastic cubes with spots on them. Treat them as such.

Superstition has no place in professional gambling. Stick to statistic-based play. Coldly throw the dice and let the odds play themselves out while keeping an eye on the game's normal volatility.

Gambler A, Gambler B, and Gambler C

Let's try and analyze the components of a winning player. Let's say we have three craps players. Gambler A plays a statistically perfect game, only playing pass line and come bets and always backing up with the full odds the casino will allow. Let's assume he never deviates from this pattern but has weaknesses in other areas. Let's say he has no money management skills at all, he is under-capitalized, and has trouble ever walking away from the table with a win or has a tendency to pull out more money when losing. He might even play with "scared" money, money he can't afford to lose. Now, let's look at gambler B. Gambler B plays an erratic game of craps. He plays pass line and come bets with odds but also the place numbers and even violates the 3% rule from time to time with hard ways, any craps or betting the "yo" occasionally. But let's also say gambler B is an extremely skilled money manager. He walks to the table well-capitalized with discretionary funds. He watches his bankroll and doesn't hesitate to pick up and leave if the dice turn sharply against him. He also has the knowledge and fortitude to recognize a hot roll and leave the table instantly when it concludes.

Gambler A will probably be able to get a lot of action for the least amount of money bet. But without any money management skills, the house's edge will surely grind him down and his losses will mount. Gambler B, while he will still most likely lose money over time because of the advantages he gives away to the house, will probably do better than gambler A. Our goal would be to become a gambler C. That is, a player who combines the best of our two hypothetical players; one who plays with statistical correctness while managing his money wisely. To put all the components of the winning player together takes knowledge, practice, discipline, and experience.

Set a Session Rule

There's no better feeling than cashing in at a table, playing right (i.e. pass line and come), then watching an endless succession of point and come numbers repeat with the 7 nowhere to be found. Similarly, the wrong side better is equally joyful when he experiences an endless succession of point 7, point 7 as his bankroll swells. But sessions rarely go so purely perfectly.

Many times I've seen players who are playing right side and panic when the dice fail to pass two or three times and quickly switch to the don't side, only to see the dice start passing! Or, if they don't know how to play don't pass (most don't) they'll simply pick-up and leave or stop betting, watching and waiting for the dice to start passing again.

Generally speaking, it is difficult to win a session when "chasing" the dice based on intuition or gut feeling. For example, let's take a pass line/come bet player who starts out and 7's out 3 times in a row, and then switches to don't pass/don't come in anticipation of the dice staying cold. At this point, after 3 losses, if he were properly capitalized to begin with he would have lost almost half of his table stake. Now, if he switches, he's really beginning a don't pass game with substantially depleted funds. This is, of course, a huge disadvantage. Furthermore, he must now rethink his game plan. He must rethink his bets, his pattern, as well as redefine his goals and redefine what he will consider a losing session. He must do all this in the middle of live play, with a crippled bank roll. This is a lot to ask even of an experienced professional!

Moreover, I assure you that a loss incurred while switching back and fourth, chasing the dice, is far more emotionally gut wrenching and regret-filled than a loss sustained when sticking to a well thought out plan that is professional in nature and is proven to offer a high degree of success.

The bottom line of all this is simply: set a session rule before becoming involved at the craps table. Select one of the following session strategies before you start:

1. All pass/come (right side)
2. All don't pass/don't come (wrong side)
3. Don't pass until the dice pass once then switch to the pass line and stay there.
4. Whatever the dice just did—do that.

Let's examine these four recommended strategies one by one.

All Pass/Come (Right Side)

This first session rule is quite straightforward. Here, you calculate the proper table stake, bet size, pattern and progression, and you engage exclusively in a right side game until the session ends, which happens when:

1. a predefined "hot roll" occurs and you play it out until the shooter "7"'s out (a win session);
2. the remaining table stake will not cover one full cycle of bets (a loss session); or
3. you see that play is fiercely against you and "short stop" the session before reaching the bottom of your table stake.

To employ this session rule, the player should prepare in every way for a right side game and look for a table that appears active and seems to be "warm" (making numbers).

All Don't Pass/Don't Come (Wrong Side)

Here, you'll calculate your play parameters, bet size, table stake, bet pattern, and bet progression and engage exclusively in a "wrong side" game until the session ends, which happens when:

1. you hit a predetermined win goal of, say, fifty percent of the original table stake, at which time you'll go on a predetermined G & E (Guarantee and Excess), socking away winnings until a hot roll comes about picking off one cycle of bets (a win session);
2. you no longer have enough money in the rails to cover one full cycle of bets(a loss session); or
3. the dice turn fiercely against you and you "short stop" the session before reaching the bottom of your bankroll.

To employ this session rule, you should prepare in every way for a don't side game and look for a table that appears somber, where the players are groaning and the dice appear cold (no passes).

All Don't Pass until the Dice Pass then Switch to Pass and Stay There

This is probably my favorite strategy but requires a bit more explanation than the previous two.

As we already know, if a point is established, the odds in fact favor the 7 showing before the point—the dice will more likely not pass. All our strategies are based around either the dice passing by repeating the point or not passing when the 7 comes before the point, all with odds. That is to say, we don't concern ourselves with natural 7's or 11's or craps 2, 3, or 12 on come out rolls.

In the strategy we are examining now, you approach a table with the assumption that the dice will do what the odds say they'll do—not pass. Here you capitalize yourself for a pass line game and begin on the don't pass line. You will continue to play don't pass as long as the table stays cold. The only difference now is that if and when the dice do pass, you then immediately switch to a pass line game and stay on the pass line until the session ends by one of the standard ending rules (i.e. hot roll, bottom of bankroll, or short stop).

Let's think about this for a moment. If we start out with a don't game and the dice start cold they may stay cold; you could conceivably end the session with a don't win never having switched to the pass side. If the dice stay cold for awhile but ultimately do heat up, then you'll be there for the hot roll, ending the session by the hot roll rule (leave when it ends).

This session rule allows you to go to the table prepared for a win with the win goals and loss limits all well defined before you commence play, while allowing a measure of responsiveness to the dice. Remember, defining wins and loses before play begins is a crucial component of long term winning.

Obviously, one might play this strategy with an occasional loss from time to time. Sometimes when you begin on the don't side, the dice pass once, causing you to switch over to pass, then begin on a cold streak. No strategy or system of play will guarantee a win every time. But, with a session rule such as this one, you're playing with a well-defined strategy that gives you a little extra felxibility to respond to the dice.

Whatever the Dice Just Did—Do That

This is a strategy that attempts to capitalize on every potential streak as it begins. Again, if we agree that one key to winning is managing streaks by maximizing gains and minimizing losses when streaks occur, then this strategy is a valuable tool in streak management. For years, many qualified professionals have recommended this strategy or strategies very similar to this.

In this approach we simply, and very mechanically, do exactly what the dice just did. If the dice passed, we make a pass line bet. If they pass again, we collect our winnings and make another pass line bet, and so on. If at any time the dice fail to pass, we then take our loss and make a don't pass bet. If the dice fail to pass again, we collect our winnings and make another don't pass bet, and so on. Let's again be clear: we're not betting on feelings and hunches. Nor are we mindlessly chasing the dice. We are very systematically reacting to what the dice have just done.

For the moment, imagine that during a session the dice experience four passes in a row and then 7 no passes. This would mean a win for our "Just did—do that" bettor. Essentially, each time the dice either pass or don't pass two or more times in a row, a win results. Now, of course, the losses would result when the dice "chop". That is to say, if the dice go on a streak of alternating pass, no pass, which does happen from time to time, then the "Just did—do that" bettor takes a loss. Nonetheless, this is a valid way to play.

When using this session rule you may want to modify your bet pattern to simply one line bet, and either take or lay double odds as you'll tend to be switching sides more often. It's a little less cumbersome to continually "make the turn," especially from the don't pass to the pass line, when two or more don't come bets remain after the point has been made, now requiring you to make a pass line bet. You may also want to consider a larger wager for your line bets as you may decide not to follow them up with come and don't come bets. You'll also need to define your win goal based on a percentage of your table stake, and then use a G & E policy and ride out whichever streak you happened to be on when the goal was attained (see section on Guarantee and Excess in chapter 8).

Similar to establishing bet patterns and progressions, effectively implementing session rules take a lot of practice, especially strategies number 3 and 4. Select one of the four session rules that most appeals to you and practice it until you feel adept and comfortable before attempting it in live play. Then, select another and practice it. The type of disciplined flexibility that comes with being comfortable with all four session rules will add depth, strength, and enjoyment to your game.

Practice makes perfect

Whatever bet patterns, progressions, and session rules you favor, it is essential that you practice in the privacy and comfort of your home if you want to make your best effort at the tables in live play. One can read many books and magazines on the game of golf, but until one puts a club in one's hands and starts hitting balls, one will not learn the game.

Action at the tables can move quickly and mistakes will be made. Remembering and keeping up with all the bets and proper odds sizes while maintaining discipline can be quite difficult, especially for the inexperienced. Here's a great idea for the beginner: for about $25 you can go to any good gaming store and buy a craps layout. Affix it to the inside of a box and "voila!" you have your own craps table. Use quarters, nickels, and pennies to represent $25, $5 and $1 chips. Run through a simple bet pattern a few times, throwing the dice and making all the correct payoffs. Then switch over to the other side. Practice implementing your favorite session rule or rules. Continue making and paying off bets while occasionally changing your bet patterns.

To make the most of these practice sessions, you must record the results. These record sheets should be very simple and should include the date, the amount bet, the starting bankroll, the bet pattern, the progression, the session rule, and the result of the session, and any comments you'd like to remember. For example, the $10 player might want to practice a straight Pass line game with double odds playing three numbers with no progression. His sheet might look like this:

Practice record sheet

Date	Bet Size	Bankroll	Pattern	Progression	Session Rule	Result
10/9	$10	$630	*rightside side 3's dbl. Odds*	*level*	*all pass*	$440

Ultimately, you should—I am tempted to say you must—
keep similar records on all your live casino play, including the
names of the casinos. Only when accurate records are kept and
available for analysis can you begin to truly understand yourself
as a player and hone your skills to best meet the casinos head on.

You must feel comfortable practicing at home before you
attempt a live session at the casino if you want the best chance
of winning.

All About Attitude

One must always be patient in gambling. Impatience and greed
combined with ignorance prove the downfall of most gamblers.
If you approach the table with the mindset, "I feel lucky and I'm
going to kill the casino tonight!" or, as I've heard so many gaming friends say, "I'm due for a win tonight so I'm going all out!"
you're only asking for disaster. The dice don't care how you feel
and nobody is ever "due" for or owed a win. The seasoned professional approaches the table with all his wits about him and
with the basic tenets of sound gaming firmly in place in his mind.
He is *prepared* for a win and equally prepared to short stop a loss
if necessary. If you begin a session determined to triple or quadru-
ple your money, odds are you're headed for disappointment.

You must be mentally flexible when challenging the tables.
You must be ready to play for twenty minutes or two hours. You
must be ready to walk away at the proper time, win or lose,
whenever that time might come. You must be ready to exercise
sound gaming policies with consistency. Unlike an athlete, a gambler's undaunted determination will have little effect on his success at the table. Successful gambling takes a very specific
mental constancy that very few people, without guidelines to
follow, will ever acheive. Work on developing this mindset.

CHAPTER TEN

As Incredible As It Sounds . . .

The longer you play casino craps, the more unusual or down-right dumbfounding events you are likely to witness. The odds of the game are quantifiable and a thorough knowledge of the statistics and percentages is the foundation of intelligent play and long-term winning.

Having said that, let's enjoy the following true story and perhaps even learn something from it.

A couple of years ago two friends of mine, let's call them Ken and Mike, and I took a weekend excursion to Las Vegas. We were staying at the Tropicana and we met another friend of ours who lives out there. His name was Rick.

We arrived on Friday morning and hooked up with our friend Rick later that afternoon. We had been gambling all after-noon, just taking breaks for food or to check out the sports book or whatever. I play craps and blackjack exclusively—I only play games in which I'm proficient, or I don't play at all. I'm not going to mindlessly make donations to the casino coffers in the name of fun and excitement. I'm there to make money. Fun and excitement are welcome byproducts of gaming but not the main thrust. Mike, on the other hand, enjoys many of the games offered, from blackjack and craps to roulette to Caribbean stud poker to slots. Rick, being that he lives in Vegas, tries to limit his play but does like the tables. Kenny is strictly a video poker enthusiast with an occasional venture at "21".

We played on into the night. I had been working on some bet progressions at the dice table most of the time and had been doing fairly well but only eking out modest gains. My buddies clearly respect my knowledge and experience at craps and marvel at my consistent winning. They ask questions, but when my answers get a little technical or involved they're off to the races looking for that quick score. I don't blame them. No one wants to go to Las Vegas for three days to hear a lecture.

It was about 11:00 P.M. Saturday night. We had been playing so much that we thought we'd take a break, drive up the strip, take in the sights, and maybe get a late supper. Rick suggested we take a ride out to the Rio. The Rio is a beautiful new casino located about one mile off the strip to the West. It stands about 30 stories high, towering over the flatlands.

The structure was as opulent as you might imagine; 117,000 square feet of gaming space. The craps tables were trimmed with striking black felts. It was obvious that this casino drew an upscale crowd. We played around a little with a few slot machines as we soaked up the atmosphere. I wasn't up to engaging in the tables at this point. It was late and it had been a long day.

At this time, Kenny approached me and told me that a friend of ours had recently been in Vegas and won several thousand dollars, mostly at the craps table. Kenny said he couldn't be sure but he thought he remembered our friend saying that he did it mostly with something called a "popped" or a "hopped" bet, or something like that. I told Kenny he was probably talking about a hop bet and that it was very unlikely that the hop bet contributed substantially to the win.

I've know Kenny for many years. He's six feet tall and weighs 245 pounds, is quite outspoken, loves to have an outrageous time, and is always the first one to escalate a situation. Most of all, he loves to take risks—just ask the I.R.S. When I intimated that the hop bet is a long-shot proposition with outrageous odds, Kenny perked up. I explained to him that it's a one-roll bet you make that wagers the next roll of the dice will come up a specific number—such as a matching pair of 2,2, or a non-matching pair like a 5,4. "What does it pay?" he queried nonchalantly, as if I didn't already know what was coming.

"Thirty to one in the generous casinos but usually only twenty-nine to one" I responded quietly, lowering my head and hoping the casino fire alarm would sound.

"Twenty-nine to one!" Kenny exclaimed. "You gotta-be kiddin' me!"

"But Kenny," I started out, "this bet gives the casino a 16.67% advantage over you. It's by far the worst bet on the table!" I called out after him, but too late. Kenny was making a beeline to the nearest dice table.

Bear in mind that Kenny knew nothing, and still knows nothing, about the game of craps. At that point he had never even stood at a dice table in his life. As he approached the table he turned toward me and waved his hand, motioning for me to come over. I accommodated. "Alright, what do I do?" he pleaded.

"Ahh...jump in a cab and go home?" I suggested.

"Come on, Rob, let's give it a try."

"Okay, okay," I said. "What number do you want to bet on?"

"How about a pair of three's?" he asked.

I looked to the standing dealer and asked what the hop bet paid. "29-1" he responded.

"29-1, Ken. Not so good," I said in one final appeal.

"Come on, come on!" he urged me, unable to take his eyes off the layout.

"Okay," I said. "See the guy sitting down?" I pointed to the boxman. "Take your bet and throw it in front of him and say, 'Hop bet on the hard six!'" Kenny produced a $100 dollar bill and threw it to the boxman.

"Cash plays!" I interjected. This let the boxman know that were not cashing in but that this represented a single bet played in cash.

"What's the bet?"

"Kenny, you're on," I said.

"Uhh . . . hop six!" Ken exclaimed.

"What?" the baffled boxman asked. Before we had a chance to answer, the shooter launched the dice into the air.

"Hard six hop'n!" I shouted in the nick of time, with the cubes still airborne.

"Bet!" the boxman responded, meaning our bet was booked and we were on.

The dice came crashing down into a pile of chips bet on the place numbers, spun around, and landed. "Six the hardway!" cried the stickman. "Pay that hop."

"Yes!!!" Kenny let loose a scream they could hear across the floor and probably across Las Vegas Boulevard. After all my caveats and warnings, Kenny hit on his first craps bet ever . . . $2,900 dollars in winnings.

With this, our friends Mike and Rick, who had been right at our side every step of the way, were jumping for joy and patting me on the back, sarcastically honoring my cautionary words of wisdom. Kenny walked away from the table with two hands full of black chips. "What do ya say, Rob, are we learning yet?" he jabbed.

"Great job, Ken. Congratulations." What else could I say? Well, the jokes went on a few minutes, and I suggested we might head back.

"Sure," Kenny said. "Right after I make one last bet."

"You're kidding," I said. "You're way ahead of the game—bank the winnings!" But the voice of reason had never influenced Kenny in the past. Why would it this time? Off again, headed for the felts.

Kenny zeroed in on a table. As we approach, he reached into his pocket and pulled out one of those black $100 dollar chips. The four of us descended on the table. Kenny, his eyes fixated once again on the multi-colored layout, asked me, "what are those magic words again".

Having lost my will to resist by witnessing that last astounding victory, I surrendered and answered, "just say 'hard six on the hop'".

Kenny threw his black chip in front of the boxman and called out "hard six on the hop"! The boxman confirmed the bet. As we waited for the shooter Kenny devilishly rotated his head towards me and made eye contact, with a grin on his face that said he knew something I didn't. This was the second roll of his illustrious craps career.

The dice landed. Another hard six. Another $2,900 dollars. Everyone at the table understood what had taken place. Wild cheers filled the air. I dropped my head in shame. My friends howled and patted me on my back in mock consolation.

As incredible as this story sounds, it didn't end there.

We jumped into our car and headed back to the Tropicana. By now it was about three o'clock in the morning. The congratulations of Kenny and the relentless ribbing of me continued, all in good fun, of course. The odds of what had just happened, hitting two hard sixes in a row, are 1,225-1.

We arrived back at our hotel and decided we'd better get some sleep. As the casino would have it, to get to the elevators we had to pass the craps pit. The action was heavy. "Yep," Kenny said, "it's about time to get some sleep". Then he flashed that devilish smile again and held up four of the Rio's gaming chips, two blacks and two greens. "But I think we have time for just one more bet, don't you?"

Back to the tables we went. Already feeling like a seasoned gamester after having rolled the dice twice in his craps career, Kenny swaggered up to the table and threw $250 dollars to the boxman and bellowed "hard six hop'n, my good man!"

"Hard six on the hop" the boxman repeated, booking the bet. The dice flew and tumbled to the layout.

As god is my witness—another hard six. At 29-1 the payoff was $7,250.

In an attempt to try to quantify what had taken place that evening, I'll put it like this: the odds of any particular pair on the dice showing on any particular throw of the dice is 35-1. The odds of having the same particular pair show on any designated three consecutive rolls, as Kenny did, are a cool 42,875-1.

By this time you might have guessed the epilogue to the

story. Kenny now figured he had found the key to the casino's vault. His whole craps career at that point consisted of three rolls, $450 dollars bet, and $13,050 in winnings. Who could blame him? But odds are a very powerful thing. Given enough time they will always play themselves out.

The next morning, we all rose and went downstairs for breakfast. All still marveled at the incredible events of the prior evening. All except Kenny, that is. Kenny was unusually quiet and devoured his breakfast at breakneck speed.

"Well, I'm done. Meet you guys in the casino" Kenny announced. And off he went. Kenny no longer needed help betting or playing. He stood at the dice table and laid down one $100 dollar bet after another. His bet pattern? You guessed it; one hop bet after another, all on the hard six.

I'm not sure exactly how much of that $13,050 dollars Kenny gave back to the casino that day. He may have given it all back, plus more. Luckily, we had to leave about 5:30 P.M. that day. On the plane ride home Kenny was subdued and would only nod his head and smile when any of us mentioned that one fabulous night in Vegas that would live in our minds forever.

What, if anything, can we learn from such a narrative? Well, it certainly underscores the wild unpredictability of dice. But it also illustrates the fact that while the dice can at any moment act crazy, if you give them enough time, they will eventually do what they're supposed to.

CHAPTER ELEVEN

Miscellaneous

Tipping

Tipping, which in casino vernacular is sometimes called "toking," is a part of gambling. Whether tipping a waitress, valet, cab driver, porter, or dealer, tipping is a personal choice influenced by a number of factors. The word T.I.P.S. is understood by many to stand for "To Insure Prompt Service". As there are good waitresses and bad waitresses, there are good dealers and bad dealers in a casino. Good performance should be rewarded and bad performance discouraged. Craps crews usually consist of four dealers—three on and one on break—work as a team and split tips. One should look over the crews on duty when deciding where to play or even whether to play at all. There are many casinos out there and many crews. You'll be interacting with the crew quite a bit when gaming, with real money at stake. Playing craps correctly and sticking to disciplined game plans is difficult enough as it is. If you find a crew or a crewmember irritating or disrespectful or maybe disinterested in the game or even his job, then not only should you not tip but you should refrain from playing altogether.

In general, dealers are hardworking people who are competent and enjoy what they're doing. When this proves to be the case they deserve a little thanks over and above their standard pay.

How and when you tip can actually have an influence on your performance as a gambler. Tipping is a personal decision. I recall once I calculated approximately how much I had tipped that year. I figured it to be several thousand dollars. I further figured that this had been too much, percentage-wise, and I have since altered my tipping accordingly. If on average we're giving a little less than a one percentage point advantage to the house, then tipping indiscriminately can easily double or triple that advantage. This is not good, performance-oriented gaming.

Different people tip at different times. Frequently you'll see people tip at the end of their gaming session. While this is appreciated by the dealers it may not be the smartest time to tip for the player. Dealers can influence your game. When things get fast and the action is heavy, it's easy to forget to make a come bet or to make an odds wager (your best bet) or even to pick up winnings! A dealer who is alert will quickly pick up your bet pattern and will tell you if he believes you've overlooked something. But the dealer will be more attentive to your game and responsive to you if you've tipped during play. If you've wait until the end of your session to tip it is quite possible that you miss out on some of this extra attention or service. Further, if a dispute should arise the dealer might look more favorably on your position if you've been tipping.

Some tip right as they begin play. This might be a bad "bet," because you might be tipping a crew that turns out to be quite disgruntled, unappreciative and or even rude. Then you might find it difficult to ask for your tip back.

I suggest this: as you approach the table, acknowledge the dealers and begin play on a positive note. If the dealers show any kind of favorable effort and attitude try and tip early—say within the first twenty rolls. From there, if one of the crew shows exceptional service and attention or perhaps catches you making an oversight—tip again. Good performance deserves reward and good dealers should be acknowledged. Finally, tip again as you leave, especially if you've won. It can be a good idea to tip as you cash out for this reason: if you are a rated player trying to earn comps (we will cover comps shortly), as you leave the table the floorman will step over and ask the dealer to estimate your average bet and length of play. If you've tipped fairly and throw a little cash down as you leave, the dealers will tend to be more "player friendly" when reporting.

How you tip is important too. You can place a bet "for the dealer" and if it wins, the dealer gets the winnings. Usually dealers know the odds. To tip by making high percentage hop bets or any sevens might not be as appreciated as bets with better odds that give the dealers a better chance at winning. Maybe make a line bet for them or a field bet. I prefer multiple roll bets—I like my tips to stay out there a while to get maximum exposure. When I feel the crew is doing a good job I like to make a couple of the ever-popular hardway bets. Despite the 9.09% to 11.1% advantages I find the dealers appreciate these bets. It also allows me to literally throw the bet out to the middle of the table and it will sit out there for a while. I don't like to keep my tips a secret.

However you choose to tip, I suggest that if you've determined the crew to be doing a good job, tip early and again as you leave. The dealers will appreciate it and this will pay dividends over time.

Comps or Complimentaries

Casino operation, like most industries, is a highly competitive business. Casinos do hold an advantage on all the bets on the table (except, of course, free odds) but if there is no money on the table, then any percent of nothing is nothing! Casinos need action and lots of it to guarantee profit. There are lightweight gamblers out there. The floors are full of them. While the casinos do appreciate this action, what they're really after is the premium players. They prize the large bettors with solid credit and they'll fight hard for them. When they find a premium player they'll try to keep him by lavishing him with perks of many sorts. These are called complimentary services, or comps for short.

As mentioned in the earlier chapters, the job of the floorman is not only to assist the players but also to rate their play. They do this with the assistance of the boxmen and the dealers. Casinos sometimes have rather elaborate systems for rating players. A player's value is usually based on two factors: time at the tables and average bet size. Moreover, the floormen will be particularly interested in the first three bets a player makes. Casinos are very tight-lipped about exactly what they are looking for and won't even tell a player exactly where he stands in terms of comps earned or what he needs to do to earn them.

If a player warrants rating, he is usually introduced to a casino host who tends to the players needs when he's not at the table—room accommodations, theater tickets, restaurant reservations, etc. A player who plays ten hours a day but who's average bet size is only $5 will probably not garnish much special attention from the hosts, especially in the larger establishments. Similarly, a player who bets a couple of hundred dollars at a time but may only spend 20 minutes or so a day at the table might turn a few heads but is not someone the casinos will go out of their way to retain. The casinos need large amounts of money to fly at tables to guarantee their cut. Keep in mind, casinos are not necessarily looking for unskilled players. They just want action, even from masterful pros. They simply want money on the table. They're confident that if there is enough money on the tables long enough, they'll get their share.

Currently, if you play with $15 bets or with twenty-five dollar chips and can play at least three hours a day, most casinos will show some interest in you. They might credit some of your room charges and meals. If you're not sure whether your action is the type a particular casino is looking for, simply call the floorman over and tell him you'd like your play to be rated. They'll need you to apply for player's card at no charge (all the casinos nowadays have them). This is a simple process that allows the casinos to track you and keep a log of your play on the computer. If you feel your play might be deserving of some comps, feel free to directly ask the floorman or host for some consideration.

One word of warning: where complimentary services are nice to receive, these services are far from "free" if you are regularly sustaining large dollar losses at the tables! I strongly suggest studying gambling for the purpose of giving you the best chance of making money over time. Don't let the prospect of earning comps influence you to play at levels that you are uncomfortable with or for periods of time you know are too long, all for the purpose of accumulating comp credits. You'll ultimately find this to be a very bad investment. Play the game the way it should be played. Increase your bet size when you feel good and ready and end your sessions in accordance with the rules of disciplined play. The complimentaries will come, and when they do they will add nicely to the enjoyment of the gaming experience. But don't make them a primary focus. They are only part of the illusion created by the casino.

Definitions

Bankroll: the total amount of money available for gambling (usually for one outing).

Boxcars: a pair of dice totaling twelve.

Cold Table: a table where the dice fail to pass shooter after shooter.

Come Out Roll: first roll of a game.

Come Roll: all rolls other than the come out roll.

Craps: the 2, 3 or 12.

Cycle: the maximum number of bets the player will have on the table at one time.

Game: the rolls thrown from the come out roll until the dice either pass or don't pass.

Guarantee & Excess (G & E): a theory in gaming where the player sets aside the majority portion of his current win (the guarantee) and resolves to risk only a small portion of the win (the excess) to ride out the current streak.

High Roller or Premium Player: one that bets large amounts of money usually for extended periods of time.

Hot Roll: an extended winning pass line roll (subject to an individual players definition).

Inside Numbers: 5, 6, 8, 9.

"Little Joe": dice totaling four.

Outing: a series of planned gaming sessions grouped together (e.g., one night at a gambling boat or 3 days in Las Vegas).

Outside Numbers: 4, 5, 9, 10.

Session: a player's play, from when he approaches a table and begins play until he stops betting and leaves.

Snake Eyes: a pair of dice totaling two.

Table Stake: the amount of money a player brings to the table and the maximum amount he'll lose at one session.

The "Yo": dice totaling eleven.